TIME GENTLEMEN PLEASE

**Village Public Houses in South
Nottinghamshire in days gone by**

BERNARD V. HEATHCOTE

I rose politely in the club and said, "I feel a little bored; will someone take me to a pub?"

Gilbert Keith Chesterton, A Ballade of an Anti-Puritan

PREFACE

Time Gentlemen Please, the well-known salutation uttered by the landlord or landlady or bar-person when the end of legal time for selling beer etc, in a public house was reached. This was at one time usually 10 or 10.30 in the evening, or 2.30 or 3.00 in the afternoon, except at lunch-time on Sundays when public houses opened between 12 and 2.00 pm. Today times are more flexible and generous. Prior to the final announcement it was traditional to call last orders after which the towel would be placed over the pumps. Opening times, on Sundays, have always been somewhat more limited and many a publican in earlier times has been prosecuted for serving customers during the period of divine service.

I have accumulated information about public houses in Nottinghamshire over a number of years, however in order to make a coherent study of such a large subject, it was necessary to limit the number of parishes and public houses to review. The ones I chose come within South Thurgarton Hundred. The reason is two-fold. Firstly the early licence records [Recognizances] 1809-26 have survived and coincidently they fall within the area in which I live.

One avenue of my research was to search the Nottinghamshire newspapers, from the beginning of the 18th century to the mid-19th century, available on microfilm in the Local Studies Library, Nottingham, where the film readers are well suited to scanning papers. I soon discovered there was an abundance of public house information, but one aspect was clear, there were very many reports of coroners' inquests, the vast majority taking place in public houses. I was therefore somewhat distracted from my initial intention of public house research and switched my focus onto recording coroners' inquests. Because of the large number available, it was necessary to limit the number to record. I chose those that were carried out by Christopher Swann, who was coroner for one of Nottinghamshire's districts from 1828 to 1866. Swann was very supportive towards the newspaper reporters and gave them access to many of his records. I found 4465 inquests reported in the three Nottingham papers. A selection of these is included and discussed in my book "Viewing the Lifeless Body".

Nevertheless I have finally written the current book on Nottinghamshire public houses in days gone by. Although I must admit this again has been somewhat delayed in the writing as I have recently published a book entitled "Vale of Belvoir Angels" which is a survey of a group of early slate headstones with characteristic features which are to be found in churchyards of the Vale and some surrounding parishes of Leicestershire, Lincolnshire and Nottinghamshire.

Over time fifty alehouses/public houses have been recorded in the 11 villages under review in this book, some closed down many years ago, others over the years, have changed their names. In addition to these premises there were a number of unnamed small beer-shops. The public house was traditionally the preserve of the male population, although there were, from time to time, a number of landladies, many of these had succeeded to the licence following the death of their husbands. It took many years before women were welcomed into the village pub, although the breweries were making some changes, introducing rooms that were acceptable to family groups and installing indoor toilets. Many pubs had a number of small rooms which would separate the various needs of customers; at a minimum a bar and a lounge. The prices were usually higher in the latter area. In the towns, some rooms were very occasionally set aside for ladies and some labelled mixed bar and others reserved for gentlemen.

Most of the village public houses, recorded in this book, would have entertained coroners' inquests, and I make no apologies for including a number in the text, and I hope the reader will find them fascinating reading.

Dedication

This book is dedicated
to the author's late wife
PAULINE FLORENCE HEATHCOTE
as a small token of appreciation
for her loving support over many years

CONTENTS

CONTENTS

COUNTY OF
Nottingham, ‹
(TO WIT.)

*A*T a ~~General~~ *special* Meeting of his Majesty's Justices of the Peace acting in and for the South Division of the County of Nottingham held at *the Shire Hall in Nottingham* in the Division and County aforesaid, on the *thirteenth* Day of September, One Thousand Eight Hundred and Twenty- *three* *a new Tenant of a House known by* *Hannah Wilson* at the Sign of *the Volunteer* in *Caythorpe* in the said *and lately occupied by Richard Wilson* Division and County, Victualler, acknowledged herself to be indebted to our Sovereign Lord the King in the Sum of *Thirty* Pounds and *Robert Heyworth* of *Caythorpe* in the said County, *Farmer* acknowledged himself to be indebted to our Sovereign Lord the King in the Sum of *Twenty* Pounds, to be levied upon their several Goods and Chattels, Lands, and Tenements, by way of Recognizance, to his Majesty's use, his Heirs and Successors, upon condition that the said *Hannah Wilson*

do and shall keep the true Assize in uttering and selling Bread and other Victuals, Beer, Ale, and other Liquors, in her House, and shall not fraudulently dilute or adulterate the same, and shall not use, in uttering and selling thereof, any Pots or other Measures that are not of full size, and shall not wilfully or knowingly permit Drunkenness or Tippling, nor get drunk in her House, or other Premises; nor knowingly suffer any Gaming with Cards, Draughts, Dice, Bagatelle, or any other sedentary Game, in her House, or any of the Outhouses, Appurtenances, or Easements thereto belonging, by Journeymen, Labourers, Servants, or Apprentices; nor knowingly introduce, permit, or suffer any Bull, Bear, or Badger-baiting, Cock-fighting, or other such sport or amusement, in any of her Premises; nor shall knowingly or designedly, and with a view to harbour and entertain such, permit or suffer Men or Women of notoriously bad fame, or dissolute Girls and Boys, to assemble and meet together in her House, or any of the Premises thereto belonging; nor shall keep open her House, nor permit or suffer any Drinking or Tippling in any part of her Premises, during the usual Hours of Divine Service on Sundays; nor shall keep open her House, or other Premises, during late Hours of the Night, or early in the Morning, for any other purpose than the reception of Travellers, but do keep good Rule and Order therein according to the purport of a Licence granted for selling Ale, Beer, or other Liquors, by Retail, in the said House and Premises, ~~for one whole Year, commencing~~ *until* on the Tenth Day of October next, then this Recognizance to be void, or else to remain in full force.

Taken and acknowledged the Day and ‹
Year aforesaid, before us, ›

Lanct Rolleston

0.1 Alehouse Licence for Hannah Wilson at the Volunteer, Caythorpe, dated 1823

I. INTRODUCTION

This book examines the history of local Public Houses [Alehouses] by reference to the villages of Bulcote, Burton Joyce, Calverton, Caythorpe, Epperstone, Gonalston, Gunthorpe, Lambley, Lowdham, Oxton and Woodborough. The location of these villages within South Nottinghamshire is shown on the map on the inside rear cover.

1. THE EARLY YEARS

Undoubtedly outlets for selling ale or beer have been established in the above villages for very many years. These premises would have originally been known as alehouses catering primarily for the needs of local working people. Initially, they were distinguished from inns which were usually large, fashionable establishments, in or on the approaches to towns, that provided food and lodging to well-heeled travellers. Another category was the tavern, smaller than the inn but whose clientele would have expected to receive wine, food and accommodation.

2. THE ALEHOUSE [PUBLIC HOUSE]

Away from towns the keeper of an alehouse/public house was often a secondary occupation, and his wife would run the alehouse during the day, while her husband carried out his established work, this pattern continued to some extent into the twentieth century. This is not to imply that women were not licensed to run public houses, they were, particularly on the death of their husbands.

In general alehouses sold only ale or beer. Ale was brewed from malt infused with water and added spices, it was fairly easy to produce but it soon deteriorated and would be drunk a short time after production. The addition of hops, to fermented malt, produced beer and this product gradually replaced ale, and by the late 1600's un-hopped ale had virtually disappeared. Beer kept better and it was more amenable to mass production. Whilst beer was more difficult to prepare than ale, home-brewing was still carried out, but the brewing industry was becoming more widely established, and a greater proportion of commercially-produced beer was being sold in alehouses. By the late 1800's, the brewers were also buying alehouses [now called public houses], and they had therefore, effectively gained control of both the production and sale of beer. It became fashionable for public houses, in an attempt to increase their status, to append the word *inn* as the suffix to their title. Similarly, they would prefix *old* or *olde* to the public house name. Today a number of commercial companies have been buying and running public houses.

Initially the alehouse was not permitted to sell wines. Spirits were of poor quality and expensive and it took many years before this state of affairs was to some extent rectified.

3. LICENSING

Until the end of the fifteenth century the administration of alehouses was under the sole control of Local Authorities. Apart from laws, to ensure the purity and reasonable prices for bread and ale, no attempt was made by Central Government to restrict the sale of alcohol. Indeed, the classification of ale with bread shows that the former was looked upon as a necessity of life. However, in 1494, during the reign of Henry VII, in an Act to restrain vagabonds, the justices were given discretionary powers to suppress alehouses. These powers were extended in 1552, by the Act of Edward VI, for persons to be bound by recognizance, and that no one should sell ale or beer without a licence, however, many small alehouse keepers, sometimes called *tipplers* or *victuallers* slipped through the net.

The regulation of the trade in alcoholic liquor originated because it was found that the free use of intoxicating drink, produced not only incapacity and disease amongst all classes, but also, among the *lower orders*, idleness and disorderly living, crimes against life and property, and even riot and rebellion. However, as previously mentioned, beer was regarded as an important commodity, it was a popular beverage at every meal, at a time when water and milk were not considered pure, and all but a small minority of the population enjoyed drinking. On the other hand, the evils of excessive drinking were so manifest, that for five hundred years successive Governments have felt compelled to do more than punish the crimes produced by drunkenness. This has resulted in numerous Acts of Parliament.

Surprisingly, an Act was passed by Parliament which relaxed the sale of alcoholic liquor, and had a marked influence on the industry: this was the Beer Act of 1830. This allowed almost any householder to sell beer, provided he or she obtained an excise licence, and so developed a two-tier system with the new beer-shops, operating alongside the fully licensed public houses. This description, beer-shop, has been used in order to differentiate it from the magisterial-controlled beerhouse which was established under the later Act of 1869. The unlicensed beer-shop could, however, only sell beer. This new legislation resulted in over 24,000 new outlets opening in England during the first year which rose to 40,000 five years later. It was not until 1869 that the 1830 Act was repealed, and once again all premises licensed to sell alcohol came under the control of the magistrates, some licensed to sell both beer and spirits [fully-licensed public houses] and others could only retail beer [beerhouses]. Many of these latter establishments would apply for full licence status in future years although in 1968 there were still three beerhouses remaining in Nottinghamshire; today there are none. This state of affairs continued until 2006, when in a new Act of Parliament (2003), the licensing of persons who wished to retail alcoholic products became the responsibility of Local Authorities. The regulation, therefore, reverted to the situation which had existed prior to 1494 and magisterial control of publicans, which had prevailed for over five-hundred years, came to an end.

Since 1494 to the present day there have been at least 60 Acts of Parliament to control the retailing of beer, cider, wine and spirits in England, Scotland and Wales. A small selection is listed in Table 1.

Table 1.

A limited selection of the Acts of Parliament dealing with Liquor Licensing

Year	Act	Content
1494	11 Hen. VII c.2	Two Justices of the Peace may reject common selling of ale
1552	5 & 6 Edw. VI c.25	For keepers of alehouses to be bound by recognizance
1623	21 Jac. I c.7	For better repressing drunkenness and restraining the inordinate haunting of inns, alehouses and other victualling houses
1729	2 Geo. II c.28	For better regulation of licences of common inns
1753	26 Geo. II c. 31	For regulating the manner of licensing alehouses and for the more easy convicting persons selling ale and other liquors without licence
1830	11 Geo. IV & 1 Wm. IV c.64	To permit general sale of beer and cider by retail in England
1869	32 & 33 Vict. c.27	To amend the law for licensing beerhouses and to make certain alterations with respect to the sale by retail of beer, cider and wine
1964	12 Eliz. II c.26 s.1	Licensing
2003	51 & 52 Eliz. c.17	Licensing

Alehouses [public houses] were often the social hub of the village, at least for the male population, for in the early years women were rarely seen as customers in these establishments. It was not until the twentieth century that attitudes began to change and gradually it became acceptable for women to join their men folk in a public house. Many of the village public houses had large rooms called *club rooms* which were used for various meetings or gatherings. These were the venues for Friendly Societies or other similar Orders; they were also used to conduct sales of land, houses, estates etc. Coroners' inquests were also held in these *club rooms*. The public areas would invariably be divided into a number of small rooms, the Plough [World's End] in Lowdham initially had four rooms and at a redevelopment in 1967 these were amalgamated into two but today there is only a single room. This is very typical of many public houses. These small rooms would often be differentiated by name, for instance, Tap room, Smoke room, Lounge, Vaults, Snug etc. Other names were more specific, the Tea room [Magna Charta in Lowdham], Luncheon room [Four Bells in Woodborough], or the Locals' room [Green Dragon in Oxton]. Many public houses would have stables and sometimes pig-sties and a yard to accommodate stage coaches [Magna Charta in Lowdham] or carrier carts where goods would be delivered. During the 19th and early 20th centuries village public houses flourished but with the advent of higher disposable incomes and the competition of other distractions, many regular clientele were tempted away from the public house. Another source of competition today is the ready availability of cheap alcoholic drinks from other retail outlets. Although the village public house is no longer predominantly the preserve of local clientele, it attracts customers who principally arrive by the motor car, from towns or their suburban areas. Nevertheless the number of patrons is far less than it was a hundred years ago. However in an attempt to entice customers to the village hostelry and to make it more friendly to family groups, they have often dispensed with the traditional wooden chairs and installed comfortable seating and more importantly many serve good quality food - the *pub meal*.

Table 2.

Number of Licensed Houses and Population prepared by the Nottinghamshire Constabulary - published in 1903

Parish	Population (1901)	Full-on licence	Beer on-licence	Beer off-licence	Average Population to every on-licence house
Bulcote	93	None	None	None	-
Burton Joyce	931	3	None	None	310
Calverton	1159	3	1	1	289
Caythorpe	232	2	None	None	116
Epperstone	362	2	None	None	181
Gonalston	128	None	None	None	-
Gunthorpe	349	2	None	None	179
Lambley	770	3	2	None	154
Lowdham	942	5	None	None	188
Oxton	455	1	2	1	152
Woodborough	722	4	1	None	144

From the middle years of the 1800's and early 1900's public houses came under pressure from two sources, the Police and the Temperance Movement. The police carried out surveys of the number of residents in a village compared to the number of outlets which were available for purchasing alcohol. In 1903 the Nottinghamshire Constabulary published their findings and the results for the parishes under review are given in Table 2. These results do not appear to clearly indicate which parishes have too many public houses per head of population. However over the next 20 years eight were compulsory closed. These were in: Calverton [Forest Tavern], Epperstone [King's Head], Lambley [White Lion], Lowdham [White Lion], Oxton [Young Oak], Woodborough [Bugle Horn, New Inn & Punch Bowl].

0.2 Police Supervision

0.3 A Warning Hand

The police also made checks on individual landlords which lead to cartoons in satirical magazines. The Temperance Movement was also very vociferous and published anti-drink articles in a number of gospel-type publications; they also sent their members out to public houses to preach the evils of drink. Both these factors had an effect and the number of public houses diminished.

II. THE LOCAL SCENE

The first indications of alehouses in the villages under review come from the Court records of the Sessions held at Newark-on-Trent during the seventeenth century. Although the name of the village is given and that of the alehouse keepers, who were indicted for committing a variety of misdemeanours, the sign of their premises, assuming they had one, is not recorded. In fact, it is not until the middle of the next century that names of village alehouses are mentioned in Court records and also in the early Nottingham newspapers. The most common reason for a person to appear before the court was for brewing or selling ale without having first obtained a Justices' Licence. The results of a search of the records show that the majority of the villages in this area were served by outlets selling ale, some licensed others not.

During the 1700's, information can be gleaned from Nottingham newspapers about alehouses and during this period their signs and the names of the licensee were often recorded. This is usually in the form of an advertisement, announcing a forthcoming sale or auction to be held on the licensed premises. The records of the Courts, in addition to reporting the prosecution of alehouse keepers, occasionally report the issuing of licences for selling ale.

It is not until the early nineteenth century that more extensive records become available; *Alehouse Recognisances* [licences] having survived between 1809 and 1826. The next surviving definitive records, for the issue of licences, do not start until 1872, and these continue with only a few missing years, until modern times. However, other alehouse or public house records can be found in trade directories, issued spasmodically in Nottinghamshire, from 1832 until 1941. The census returns for the years, 1841, 51,61,71,81,91,1901 & 1911, and baptismal records, which from 1813, feature the father's surname and occupation, provide other background information about publicans and their families. In recent times, electoral rolls can often be useful. During the 19th century, Coroners' Inquests concerning local deaths were often held in public houses. The reports published in the press often give us an insight into local conditions and a number have been selected for inclusion in the text.

From these records a picture of the individual public house and its owners and licensees has been built up.

1. BULCOTE

Only one public house has been definitely identified in Bulcote; this went by the name of the Unicorn or occasionally, the Unicorn's Head. It is first recorded in 1811 but it may well have existed at an earlier date. In 1726 four

licences were issued for alehouses in the parish of Burton Joyce cum Bulcote and it is feasible that one these alehouses may have been in Bulcote. However, the Unicorn had a short life, for by 1864 it had closed its doors, but the reason for this abrupt end to this hostelry is not known. The building survives to this day. A list of the licensees is given in Table 3.

1.1 Ivy Cottage [the former Unicorn Inn in Bulcote] from a postcard c.1900

Table 3.

Licensees of the Unicorn in Bulcote

Period	Licensee	Period	Licensee
c.1811	John Nickall	1820 to c.1843	John Slater
1812 to 1820	Joseph Hingley	c.1843 to c.1864	Richard Allwood

In January 1812 the Inn was offered for sale at the Wheat Sheaf public house in Burton Joyce[1]. It was about this time that Joseph Hingley became the new occupant of the Unicorn. Although the size of the property is not recorded it included a barn, stable, brew-house with a malt kiln and other out-buildings, yard and gardens standing in two roods [half a statute acre].

A number of sales of property and meetings of the Nottingham Order of Odd Fellows were held at the Unicorn.

On Monday the 24th June 1844, the Nottingham United Imperial Order of Odd Fellows, Lodge No. 4, held their anniversary at Bulcote, at Mr. R. Allwood's the sign of the Unicorn's Head, when the Lambley band was in attendance. They walked in procession to Burton Joyce, where the Rev. J. Rolleston delivered an appropriate sermon. They then walked back to Bulcote, where a sumptuous dinner was provided. When the cloth was removed, several loyal toasts were drunk, and the afternoon passed off very merrily. They were regaled with supper, after which toasts and health's were drank, songs sang, and talks told, till a late hour[2].

Four coroners' inquests were held at the Unicorn between 1831 and 1861 [Miscellany Table 1.]. An example is summarised below.

Concealing Birth: *On Wednesday the 11th April 1849 an inquest was held at the Unicorn Inn, Bulcote, before C. Swann, gent., coroner, over the body of a male infant. On Tuesday afternoon, a search was made in the soil of a privy for the body of a child, of which it was supposed a cook in the service of Mr. Holgate, had been delivered. It was found. The mother acknowledged that she believed the child was born alive, but she denied having laid hands on it. Mr. Davison, surgeon, of Carlton, made a post-mortem examination of the body of the deceased and was of the opinion that the child was born alive, but that its death was caused partly from haemorrhage and partly by suffocation, in consequence of being under the bed clothes and no assistance rendered to it. Most of the evidence was quite unfit for publication. Verdict: That the deceased child died from suffocation and haemorrhage for want of proper care and attention at the time of its birth, arising from the inability of its mother to render him assistance. The mother of the child, Mary Foster, was committed to jail for concealing the birth.*

From the foregoing it is clear that the Unicorn was a substantial property with a sufficiently large room to accommodate meetings and coroners' inquests. Additionally, the licensee was able to provide food for his guests.

2. BURTON JOYCE

Virtually nothing is known of alehouses in Burton Joyce before the 17th century, apart from a brief reference in 1494, when the Mayor of Nottingham and his entourage stopped for ale on their way back from Lincoln[3]. The earliest definitive record that I can find was in the year 1609, when William Ireland was indicted at the Quarter Sessions at Newark, for refusing to entertain a traveller. Three years later a carpenter called, James Tomlynson, was discharged from keeping an alehouse, because his house was disorderly. In 1617, he was again before the Court, for brewing without a licence to do so, and in 1630 he was prosecuted for selling ale above the statutory price. Also in 1630, another victualler in Burton Joyce, Peter Green, was indicted for the same offence. In 1726, four persons were granted alehouse licences, in the parish of Burton cum Bulcote; they were, Valentine Stapleton, Thomas Lowe, Eliza Gee and Joseph Dickson. Later, in 1774, Val. [Valentine] Stapleton featured in the Nottingham press when his alehouse, whose sign is given as the Queen's Head, was the venue for the sale of land However, by 1823 it had ceased to be a public house, and was offered for sale as a dwelling as part of an estate. The position of the Queen's Head in Burton Joyce is not known.

To be sold by auction: *At the house of Val. Stapleton, being the sign of the **Queen's Head**, in Burton Joyce, in the County of Nottingham, on Friday the 19th day of August instant [1774], between the hours of two and four in the afternoon. Three closes of rich meadow or pasture ground in Burton Joyce, aforesaid, containing together about eighteen acres, now in the occupation of Mr John Cooper.*

During the 19th century there were three public houses in Burton Joyce: the Cross Keys, the Swan & Salmon [later renamed Lord Nelson] and the Wheat Sheaf. They all exist at the time of writing. There is a brief reference to a beer-shop opening in Burton Joyce, under the Sale of Beer Act of 1830, when in 1863, Matthew Alvey was indicted for allowing drunkenness in his house, but the case was dismissed. All the other outlets were fully licensed public houses able to sell beer and spirits.

Cross Keys

This public house appears to have existed from about the early 1830's. It remained in local ownership usually by the tenant until 1891 when it was sold to Edward Wheeler Field who was described as a brewer of Nottingham. Seven years later it was purchased by The Nottingham Brewery Company passing to Tennant Bros. Ltd. in the 1960's. The present owner is the Laural Pub Company, Dunstable. In 1872 it was described as having a bar, tap room and parlour and stabling for three horses. The annual value was £18.

2.1 Cross Keys, 1997

Table 4.

Licensees of the Cross Keys in Burton Joyce

Period	Licensee	Period	Licensee
c.1830 to c.1836	John Ashwell	1900 to 1905	William Doughty
c.1836 to c.1841	John Butler	1905 to 1927	William Adkin
c.1841 to c.1847	Edwin Wood	1927 to 1934	George Harry Hewitt
c.1847 to c.1850	Richard Slater	1934 to 1940	William Worthington
c.1850 to c.1852	Edward Slater	1940 to 1944	Joseph Francis Hannigan
c.1852 to c.1854	William Cumberland	1944 to 1946	May Blossom Hannigan
c.1854 to 1886	John Hogg	1946 to 1968	Joseph Francis Hannigan
1886 to 1896	Frederick Hogg	1968 to 1976	Louis Ernest Bradshaw
1896 to 1897	William Arthur Cragg	1976 to 1983	Rupert Jesse Haywood
1897 to 1898	Harold Cragg	1983 to 1992	Dennis Church
1898 to 1900	Thomas Page	1992 to	Alan R. Duriez

Thomas Page who was the landlord of the Cross Keys, 1898 to 1900, came to Burton Joyce from York where he had been a publican in that city. It seems that he treated his wife with great cruelty and she petitioned for, and received, dissolution of her marriage. They were living at the Manchester Inn in York. After his divorce, Page came to Burton Joyce, bringing with him a girl who had been one of his servants and it appears that she had been the source of trouble with his wife[4]. *[No doubt this proved a good source for gossip in the village!]*

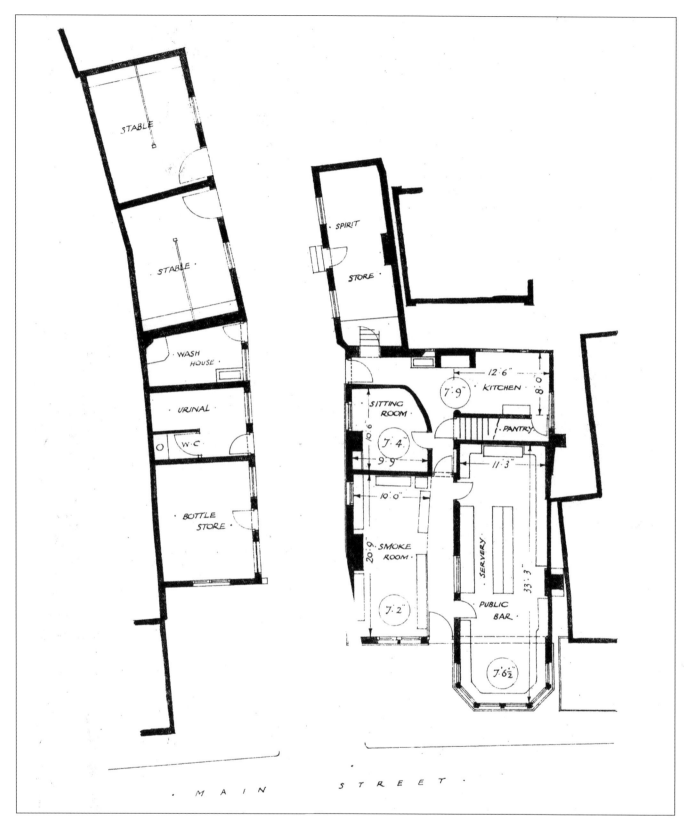

Plan 1 Ground Floor of the Cross Keys, dated 10th April 1926

A former licensee of the Cross Keys, Frederick Hogg, died very suddenly in January 1901, five years after he relinquished control of the Inn to work as a barman, and an inquest was held at the Wheat Sheaf.

Sudden Death at Burton Joyce: *The sudden death of Frederick Hogg formed the subject of a coroner's inquest held by Mr. Whittingham at the Wheat Sheaf on Saturday the 26th January 1901. His wife, Annie Hogg, said her husband was 42 years old and a barman. He retired as usual on Thursday night and about four o'clock next morning complained about a pain in his stomach and she went downstairs. He was found lying on the dairy floor. He died* *a few minutes later in his daughter's arms. Deceased had been away from home all week and was not sober when he went to bed on Thursday. Dr. Frazer attributed death to syncope [loss of consciousness] accelerated by the intemperate habits of Frederick Hogg[5].*

The Cross Keys was of sufficient size to accommodate seven coroners' inquests between 1836 and 1861 [Miscellany Table 1.]. An example is summarised below.

Death from Natural Causes: *On Wednesday the 20th January 1836 an inquest was held at the house of Mr. John Butler, the Cross Keys, Burton Joyce, on view the body of Elizabeth Dickinson aged nine weeks. The deceased's mother died a few days after she was born, when the child was placed with a Mrs. Allcock to nurse. When it had been there a fortnight, the father took it home and his daughter nursed it. The deceased was a very weak and ailing child. On Friday the father went out and left the child in the care of his daughter, intending not to return until Monday. The little girl was in the habit of feeding the deceased with bread and milk but the food was too heavy for its stomach. On Sunday night she slept with the deceased and when she got up she found the infant asleep but about 10 o'clock she went up and found the child was dead. Godfrey's cordial had been administered to the infant since she came from Mrs. Allcock and latterly it had a teaspoonful and a half every night. A neighbour gave evidence that the deceased had been well-treated by her sister. Verdict: That the deceased died of natural causes, and that her death was accelerated by having improper diet, and too large a quantity of Godfrey's cordial administered to her, and for want of proper care and attention.*

The Cross Keys has always been a popular public house and it is interesting to read the childhood reminiscences of local people and of two former licensees, Joseph & May Hannigan [1940–68] published in Burton Joyce & Bulcote Remembered[3]. A surviving ground floor plan of the Cross Keys dated 1926 [Plan 1. page 7.] shows that at this time there were three public areas, a servery, smoke room and public bar in addition there was a large room at the rear undoubtedly used for holding meetings etc. Also two stables had survived although these were shortly to be demolished. It seems very likely that the layout was little changed, from that recorded in the previous century. Additions and refurbishment to the Cross Keys, in the mid-1960's took place, and it was at this time the adjoining building, the former public house known as the Wheat Sheaf was demolished to form a car park for the Cross Keys. Twenty years later, the three small rooms were converted into a single bar, and this is the arrangement that the current landlord, Alan Duriez, inherited when he came to the Cross Keys from the Gregory public house in Radford in 1992.

2.2 Cross Keys Burton Joyce c.1896

Lord Nelson [formerly the Swan & Salmon]

2.3 Lord Nelson 1997

The first reference I have found to this public house was in the Nottingham Journal newspaper of July 1808. However, it is certainly older than this and it may be that one of the persons recorded as innkeepers in Burton Joyce in the 17th and 18th centuries were living at the Swan & Salmon. Situated close to the River Trent it would have been in an advantageous position.

Valuable Oak Timber *Growing in Burton and East Howe Wood in the parish of Burton-Joice, in the County of Nottingham, to be sold by auction at the house of Mr. John Blatherwick, the Sign of the Swan-and-Salmon, in Burton-Joice, on Tuesday the 19th day of July next* [1808], *at ten o'clock in the forenoon*[6].

The name changed from the Swan and Salmon to the Lord Nelson about 1841 when Richard Thorpe became its innkeeper. In the 19th century the Inn was described as having stabling for eight horses, a bar, tap room and two club rooms with an annual value of £18. During 1846, the Nottingham to Lincoln railway line was being constructed as it passed through Burton Joyce; the Lord Nelson Inn was a place frequented by the labourers.

Burton Joyce – *This village was in a complete uproar on Wednesday night week in consequence of a number of railway labourers who had been drinking at Mr. Thorpe's the Nelson Inn, quarrelling. From high words the navvies soon proceeded to blows, when in the mêlée one poor man, who was deaf and dumb, had his shoulder dislocated and was otherwise seriously injured*[7].

2.4 Lord Nelson, Burton Joyce c.1900

A well-known and respected lady in Burton Joyce was Mrs. Agnes E. Gee who was the landlady of the Lord Nelson for 21 years from 1933 to 1954. An advertisement of 1936 reads that she catered for parties and had the facilities of a snack bar and a spacious car park. This was part of a growing trend to widen the appeal of a number of village public houses to attract clientele over the traditional local trade.

Table 5.

Licensees of the Lord Nelson [formerly the Swan & Salmon] in Burton Joyce

Period	Licensee	Period	Licensee
c.1808 to c.1830	John Blatherwick	1921 to 1933	Annie Litchfield
c.1830 to c.1841	Richard Clarke	1933 to 1954	Agnes E. Gee
c.1841 to c.1864	Richard Thorpe	1954 to 1956	John A. Bent
c.1864 to c.1871	Elizabeth Thorpe	1956 to 1960	William Charles Harrison
c.1871 to 1879	Alfred Shaw	1960 to 1969	Albert Barnes
c.1879 to 1896	John Barnes	1969 to 1981	George Robertson Baird
1896 to 1900	Sarah Barnes	1981 to 1984	Robert Parker McGarrity
1900 to 1905	Arthur Knight Westwick	1984 to 1985	Kevin Brent Battersby
1905 to 1909	Thomas Gillson	1985 to 1986	Alan Heeley
1909 to 1912	Thomas Stevenson	1986 to 1988	Trevor Price
1912 to 1916	Martha Booth	1988 to 1990	Nigel Bramley
1916 to 1917	William Edward Sheppard	1990 to 1998	Kevin J. Pritchett
1917 to 1921	William Lacey	1998 to	Philip Webb & Sally Ann Epton

The club rooms in the Lord Nelson [Swan & Salmon] would have been used for meetings and for holding coroners' inquests and between 1831 and 1862 ten were held [Miscellany Table 1.]. An example is shown below.

In the overwhelming number of recorded verdicts of inquests, where it stated that the deceased took his or her own life, a rider was added that the person was of unsound mind at the time. This verdict had very important connotations, for it meant that in an age of strong religious fervour, the burial of the person could be performed with all the attendant rites. Only on three occasions, was a verdict of suicide reached in Christopher Swann's court, when it was stated that the person was of sound mind. This was called `felo-de-se' and then the coroners were obliged to command that the burial should take place at night without any of the normal religious rites. One such verdict was reached in Burton Joyce, at an inquest held at the Swan & Salmon on the body of Hannah Spyby. The deceased was a servant of the then inn keeper, Richard Clarke, and she hanged herself in the public house. Assuming that the burial took place in Burton Joyce I cannot find any record in the parish registers.

Suicide [Felo-de-se]: *An inquest was held on Friday 14th February 1833, at the Swan, Burton Joyce, on view of the body of Hannah Spyby, aged 23 years. The deceased had been a servant to Mr. Richard Clarke [the landlord] for nearly three years. About five years ago she had a child by a man called Iliffe, residing at Lambley, but she used to complain that she had not enough money for its support. Her manners were generally lively and she expressed a strong attachment for Iliffe. For the past week she had appeared more thoughtful and got up as usual on Wednesday morning. Mr. Clarke's daughter heard a chair fall and went down the stairs and found the deceased hanging by the neck in the kitchen. Mr. Billings, surgeon, examined her and ascertained that she was six months advanced in pregnancy. The jury returned a verdict of felo-de-se and the body of the deceased was to be buried, the same night, between the hours of nine and twelve without the usual service of the interment of the dead.*

Wheat Sheaf

This public house existed in Burton Joyce from at least the early part of the 19th century. The original site was adjacent to the Cross Keys in the Main Street but on the 6th March 1937 permission was granted for the house to be

2.5 Wheat Sheaf 1997

re-located to a site on the new by-pass road in Burton Joyce. In the 19th century the Nottingham Independent Order of Odd Fellows [Lodge 3] routinely met at the Wheat Sheaf.

On Monday 5th April 1847 The Nottingham Order of Odd Fellows held their fourteenth anniversary at Mr. John Hubbard's, the Wheat Sheaf Inn At half-past ten o'clock, the members walked in procession to church, headed by the Lambley band, when the Rev. Mr. Wicks, curate at Gedling, preached an appropriate sermon. After the service they perambulated the village till one o'clock, when they returned to their lodge, where a good substantial dinner awaited their arrival, and to it they did ample justice. The health of the Queen, and of neighbouring gentlemen, who kindly contributed every year to the Lodge, and other toasts, were received with much applause. The whole meeting passed off with great mirth[8].

Other local groups also held their meetings at the Wheat Sheaf.

On Monday 1st June 1845, the members of the sick club of the Wesleyan Chapel Burton Joyce held their second anniversary at Mr. John Hubbard's the Wheat Sheaf Inn. At two o'clock, the members and several farmers of the village sat down to a substantial dinner. The cloth having been drawn, the health's of the neighbouring gentlemen was drunk, with thanks for their liberal donations. The day was spent in mirth and conviviality[9].

2.6 Original position of the Wheat Sheaf next to the Cross Keys in the Main Street c.1900

The Wheat Sheaf was the largest of the Burton Joyce inns, in 1872 there was stabling for five horses and it had eight rooms four of them open to the public the annual value was £35. In this year, it was owned by Mrs. Mary Ann Wilkinson, who was described as a widow living in Granby. By 1884, it had been purchased by the then tenant, Edward Slater. Slater kept the Wheat Sheaf for 29 years from 1876 to 1905. At the time of the 1881 census he was unmarried aged 31 years living with his sister who was his house-keeper. However, he soon married and by 1891 he had four children and his sister appears to have been demoted to general servant. Finally in 1905 this inn ceased to be in private ownership and it was leased to Hansons Ltd., Kimberley, Brewers, and in the 1960's it was acquired by Home Brewery Co. Ltd., Daybrook passing to Scottish & Newcastle in 1997. In this year the Wheat Sheaf opened, after an extensive refurbishment, as a Chef and Brewer Inn.

Table 6.

Licensees of the Wheat Sheaf in Burton Joyce

Period	Licensee	Period	Licensee
c.1811 to c.1841	Samuel Taylor	1938 to 1939	Sam Dexter Mason
c.1841 to c.1845	Phoebe Taylor	1939 to 1940	May Mason
c.1845 to c.1861	John Hubbard	1940 to 1941	Jacob Underwood
c.1861 to c.1872	William Hubbard	1941 to 1953	Harry Underwood
c.1872 to 1876	John Blatherwick	1953 to 1960	Edward Frederick. Bucher
1876 to 1905	Edward Slater	1960 to 1961	Ronald Franklin
1905 to 1907	William Paulson	1961 to 1962	Cecil Wyler
1907 to 1908	Alfred Jennings	1962 to 1965	Maurice Bertram Lees
1908 to 1910	Harriett A. Goodacre	1965 to 1980	Alex Henry Meads
1910 (08) to 1910 (11)	Walter Ernest Brewster	1980 to 1988	Jeffrey Sale
1910 (11) to 1913	Walter Tom Bonser	1988 to 1989	David Andrew Collins
1913 (02) to 1913 (07)	Betsy Fisher	1989 to 1991	Clive Brian Buxton
1913 (07) to 1915	Eliza Tilley	1991 to 1993	Barry Stephen Jackson
1915 to 1917	Frederick Cooper	1993 to 1996	Jon Alan Cole
1917 to 1925	Francis A. Taylor	1996 (01) to 1996 (04)	Barry George Vanes
1925 to 1929	Joy Frederick Gilbert Hollis	1996 (04) to 1997	Alan George Bloomer
1929 (02) to 1929 (08)	Louise Frances Hollis	1997 to 2000	Magnus Charles Charleston
1929 (08) to 1930	Harry Paulson	2000 to 2001	Wendy Payne
1930 to 1938	Bernard Paulson	2001 to 2005	Philip John Beale
		2005 to	William John Allan Gill

Between 1828 and 1864 six coroners' inquests were held at the Wheat Sheaf [Miscellany Table 1.]. An example is given below.

On Thursday the 31ˢᵗ July 1828 an inquest was taken at the Wheat Sheaf, Burton Joyce, on view of the body George Mason, aged seven years, the son of a widow of that place, with a numerous family. John Baxter, Mr. Padley's post-boy, about a mile from Burton Joyce, saw the deceased get up on the step behind the Newark coach and ride with his face towards the coach. He had got down twice to let another little boy ride. A witness warned him of the danger, and he promised to get down, but on getting up the third time he put his foot through the wheel, which whirled him round once and then passed over his belly; he got up and ran about five yards, when he dropped. The witness shouted out and the deceased was picked up and put inside the coach. Mr. Billings, surgeon of Lowdham, said that the left leg and his side were bruised and the lowest rib broken and the viscera so much crushed by the weight of the wheel passing over him to have caused a speedy death. Verdict: Accidental death.

3. CALVERTON

There is clear evidence that by 1630, an alehouse was established in Calverton, for it has been noted, from the records of the Quarter Sessions, that three alehouse keepers, Francis Cooper, William Warton and Charles Wilson, were prosecuted for selling ale above the statutory price. Later in the century, others were indicted for brewing ale for sale without having first obtained a licence, and some for keeping disorderly houses. During the next century, surviving records show that alehouse licences were granted to Robert Marriott, John Birth, William Smith, John Bush and John Cooper. By the mid-1700's signs, of the alehouses in Calverton, were being mentioned in the newspapers. During the eighteenth century, the names of four public houses are recorded in the Nottingham papers, Abraham's Hutt, Queen's Head, Admiral Rodney and White Lion. However the last record of the Queen's Head was in 1773 and it may have changed its name to either the Admiral Rodney or the White Lion. The Admiral Rodney appears to be the most likely, for in 1773, both the White Lion and the Queen's Head are mentioned in the local press.

Admiral Rodney

This inn existed in the village from at least 1783, it had been named the Admiral Rodney in recognition of the English Admiral [1st Baron George Brydges Rodney] who was best known for his commands in the American War of Independence; particularly his victory over the French at the battle of Saintes in 1782. Prior to 1783, it is possible that the Admiral Rodney public house may have been called the Queen's Head.

To be sold by auction: *On Friday afternoon the 4th of April 1783, between the hours of two and five at the sign of the Admiral Rodney at Calverton in the County of Nottingham.* [Details of a freehold estate are given.][10]

In 1784, George Beck, late of the parish of Calverton, was found guilty of stealing two handkerchiefs the property of George Smith, the then tenant of the Admiral Rodney. For this offence Beck was committed to the House of Correction at Southwell, and in this town, he was publicly whipped in the Market Square until his body was bloody[11].

By 1796, Thomas Wood had been granted the licence, but three years later he and William Mitchell of the White Lion public house were both convicted of *suffering tippling* [allowing drinking] in their respective houses on a Sunday. They were each required to pay a fine of 10s. [50p], these monies to be used for the relief of the poorest persons in the Parish of Calverton[12]. Thomas Wood remained at the Admiral Rodney, until his death in 1814, and was then succeeded by his wife, Ann Wood; she ran the public house until 1823.

In 1789, the Admiral Rodney was offered for sale and in 1795 the then innkeeper, Thomas Clarkson left the public house to go to the Hare & Hounds in Nottingham and the house was again offered for sale.

To be sold by auction: *All that good accustomed Inn or public house known by the sign of the Admiral Rodney; with a very eligible bake-house, sheds and other conveniences suitable for a baker; together with a good stable, outbuildings, yard and appurtenances thereto adjoining, situate in Calverton, now in the occupation of Thomas Clarkson[13].*

Thomas Clarkson *of the Admiral Rodney public house in Calverton having taken the Hare & Hounds public house in Nottingham begs to inform his friends and public that he is entirely removed from Calverton to Nottingham where he intends to continue the Baking Business and will be glad to serve his customers with Feast Cakes as usual[14].*

It is clear from the foregoing that the Admiral Rodney at this time was also in business as a bakery.

In 1872, the licensee of the Admiral Rodney was Samuel Turton, and Christopher Beckitt, a farmer in Calverton, was the owner. The Admiral Rodney was by now a substantial property, having 10 rooms, five of which were open to the public; in addition there was stabling for 10 horses. The annual value was £19. However in 1890, William Henry Hutchinson, Brewer of Basford acquired the premises, [in 1908 this firm became the Home Brewery]. After a succession of licensees [Table 7.] this inn survives in Calverton today.

There were 18 coroners' inquests held at the Admiral Rodney, between 1828 and 1864, of these 10 were in children less than nine years of age. Three adults took their own lives, two died in accidents and three died from natural causes [Miscellany Table 1.]. An example is given on page 13.

Table 7.

Licensees of the Admiral Rodney in Calverton

Period	Licensee	Period	Licensee
c.1783 to c.1789	George Smith	1929 to 1935	John William Northage
c.1789 to c.1796	Thomas Clarkson	1935 to 1936	Elijah Tomlinson
c.1796 to 1814	Thomas Wood	1936 to 1955	Harry Wallace Holmes
1814 to 1823	Ann Wood	1955 to 1966	William Peck
1823 to c.1831	Christopher Beckett	1966 to 1967	Gordon Barry Pickering
c.1831 to c.1843	William Ward	1967 to 1976	Stanley Ross
c.1843 to c.1845	Henry Barrowcliffe	1976 to 1982	Colin Graham Bramhill
c.1845 to c.1861	William Baguley	1982 to 1989	Thomas Ambrose Mills
c.1861 to c.1870	John Yealand	1989 to 1993	Ian Robert MacDiarmid
c.1870 to c.1871	Cornelius Hind	1993 to 1996 (06)	Roland Smith
c.1871 to. 1876	Samuel Turton	1996 (06) to 1996 (11)	Vicki Honeysett
1876 to 1908	Richard Lee	1996 (11) to 1997 (07)	Steven John Waller
1908 to 1915	Frances Lee & Francis Fisher	1997 (07) to 1997 (12)	Derek Taylor
1915 to 1917	William E. Ward	1997 (12) to 1998	Derek Taylor & James
1917 to 1918	William Coxon		William Twells
1918 to 1922	Richard D. Worthington	1998 to 2002	Ian Michael Wyld
1922 to 1925	Edwin Alfred Reddall	2002 to 2003	Mark David Truman
1925 to 1929	Edwin Ernest Reddall	2003 to	Valerie Burns & Mark David Truman

Suicide – Insanity: *An inquest was held at the Admiral Rodney in Calverton, on Monday 6th October 1828, on view of the body of Mary Rounsevell aged about 33 years. She was one of the domestic servants of Sir John Coape Sherwood. From the evidence of the housekeeper, she went into the room of the deceased on Saturday morning, about eleven o'clock, and found her lying on the floor with her throat cut. Her head was against the towel-horse, there was a quantity of blood on the floor, and on her clothes. The looking glass was also covered with blood, and a razor was lying on the table close by. The witness and a footman, attempted to stop the bleeding with cobweb and fungus, but in vain. It appears that from several other witnesses that the deceased had been in an agitated state for some time. Apparently a valet of Sir John had proposed marriage to her but he had now left the house and he had not contacted her and this had caused her to be extremely upset. Robert Thomas Foster, surgeon of Southwell, said he was sent for by Lady Sherbrooke on the previous Thursday, to visit the deceased. He said her general health was good but she was obviously very distressed about Mr. Pessel, the valet, and she didn't know what to do. No improper intercourse had passed between them. He recommended that Lady Sherbrooke should have her watched. He was sent for again on Saturday morning and found the body as previously described. He supposed at first that she was dead but he then noticed that she was breathing and a quantity of frothy blood issued from the cut windpipe. However, she died in a few minutes and he had no doubt that she inflicted the wound herself with the razor on the table. The windpipe was cut through but the carotid artery was not severed. In his opinion she died from loss of blood and from suffocation produced by blood passing into the windpipe. Verdict: Insanity.*

3.1 Admiral Rodney 1933

A number of plans have survived detailing alterations to the Admiral Rodney, the earliest is dated 20th September 1937 but at this time changes were relatively minor. A more substantial change was carried out 1953-58, when the building was extended, to give its present-day external appearance. Internally the smoke room and tap room were enlarged and re-named as the lounge and public bar. The plan of the ground floor is reproduced below [Plan 2.]. The club room was however situated on the first floor [this plan survives but is not illustrated] and would have been the venue for meetings and the coroner's inquests.

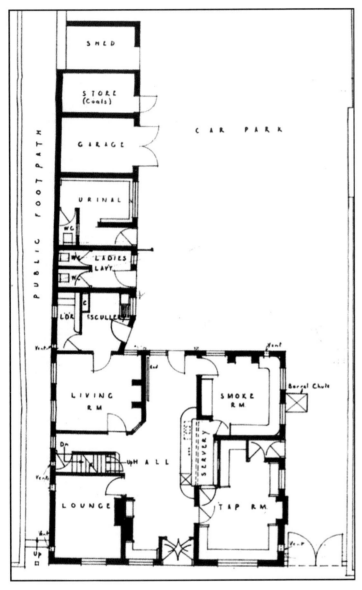

Shortly after the renovations were undertaken in 1958, so as to provide additional space, a sketch of the interior of the new lounge bar was made. A visitor at the time reported that the Admiral Rodney had a homely atmosphere, and the then landlord, William Peck, was able to provide sandwiches and snacks. There was also a large car park created.

Plan 2 Ground Floor of the Admiral Rodney, dated July 1953

3.2 The Lounge of the Admiral Rodney in 1958

Cherry Tree

The Cherry Tree is a twentieth century public house, and was opened in December 1959, in Collyer Lane, primarily to serve the population of the new housing development in this area of the village. The original building plans have survived and the ground floor plan is reproduced below. The Cherry Tree is an unusual name for a public house; however there is another one at West Drayton. At one time it had an inn sign depicting a landscape with a cherry tree. Changes in licensees are listed in Table 8. Andrew Round who was landlord of the Cherry Tree for six years, from 1965 to 1971, left to take the licence of the Four Bells in Woodborough [Table 37.]. He came into the licensed trade after being a sales representative for Hoover Ltd. The assembly room, similar

3.3 Cherry Tree 1998

to the club room in the older public houses, has been used for a variety of events over the years. It has featured musical evenings with live bands and discotheques. It has also been regularly used for local weddings, anniversaries, birthdays etc. However, at the time of writing, the Cherry Tree has been demolished.

Table 8.

Licensees of the Cherry Tree in Calverton

Period	Licensee	Period	Licensee
1959 (12) to 1960	Richard Chester	1980 to 1981	Brian Walter Langsdale
1960 to 1961	Horace Morton	1981 to 1982	Albert Roy Thompson
1961 to 1963	William Henry Mercer	1982 to 1986 (02)	Russell Cleaver
1963 to 1964	Jack Rhodes	1986 (02) to 1986 (04)	Gary John Sherwood
1964 to 1965	John Kelly	1986 (04) to 1990	David Terry
1965 to 1971	Andrew Round	1990 to 1991 (01)	Roy Crashley
1971 to 1976	Kevin Bede McPadden	1991 (01) to 1991 (04)	Garry William Toas
1976 to 1980	John Michael Alls	1991 (04) to 2001	Michael Neil Rippon
		2001 to	Michael Neil Rippon & Anthony John Wyatt

The plan below shows that the Cherry Tree had two public rooms, a large bar and a smaller Smoke room but additionally the very large assembly room with a stage.

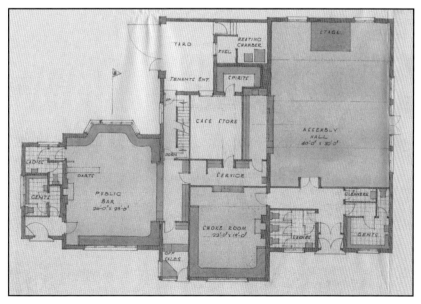

Plan 3 Ground Floor of the Cherry Tree dated 12th January 1957

Forest Tavern

About 1851, Thomas Watson a Cottager in Calverton, opened his premises in the Main Street on the outskirts of the village, as a beer-shop under the terms of the Beer Act of 1830. He ran this business for the next twenty years. In 1872, after the repeal of the above Act, a justice's licence was granted to the then licensee, Samuel Turton and the Forest Tavern became a licensed beerhouse i.e. not able to sell spirits. After a succession of owners and licensees [Table 9.], in 1910, the Home Brewery obtained the lease of the premises. However, on the 12th February 1920 this beerhouse was closed as the authorities were of the opinion that Calverton, with a population of about 1100 inhabitants, had too many outlets, for the sale of alcoholic drink. In addition to this beerhouse, there were four licensed premises. Of these, three were fully licensed houses, the Gleaners Inn – 1000 yards away; the White Lion – 520 yards away; the Admiral Rodney – 320 yards away. Also there was, nearby, premises which had an off-licence for the sale of beer, wines and spirits. The Forest Tavern was small, having three rooms for use by the public, a bar – 10ft. by 4½ft., a tap room – 10½ft. square

3.4 Former Forest Tavern, Calverton, 2002

and an upstairs club room – 30ft. by 14ft. The entrance passage to the house was restricted to 3ft. At the time of its closure the licensee was Hannah Wright [widow of John Wright]. The owner was John Smith Watson of Basford and the lessees, the Home Brewery Company Ltd., with the Ecclesiastical Commissioners registered as persons interested in the premises as Lords of the Manor. Compensation was paid to affected parties on the 20th March 1920.

Table 9.

Licensees of the Forest Tavern beerhouse in Calverton

Period	Licensee	Period	Licensee
c.1851 to c.1870	Thomas Watson	1902 to 1916 (02)	Samuel Mills
c.1870 to c.1872	Samuel Turton	1916 (02) to 1916 (04)	Esther Mills
c.1872 to 1880	Timothy Turton	1916 (04) to 1919	John Wright
1880 to 1901	Robert Parker	1919 to 1920 (02)	Hannah Wright
1901 to 1902	Rhoda Parker		

Gleaners

The Gleaners was originally a beer-shop, the first definitive record was in a deed of lease in 1835[15], but most probably it had existed one or two years earlier. At this time, the Gleaners was owned by George Windle, a builder, who leased it to John Collyer, a joiner and builder, in Calverton. The lease also included the adjoining land of about two acres. A group of surviving cottages had been erected on nearby land in 1834 [now known as Windle's Square]. Collyer who already occupied the Gleaners in 1835 ran the Gleaners until about 1860. On the 1861 census for Calverton it was listed as the "Gleaner Girl", but this was most likely a transcription error, on the part of the enumerator, although it was sometimes referred as the Gleaner. It was still a

3.5 Gleaners 1998

beer-shop run by William Cummins [aged 40, born in Scotland]. By 1872, the house was registered as a licensed beerhouse, now owned by John Collier. At this time William Wibberley held the justice's licence. The Gleaners had nine rooms, of which four were open to the public and in addition, stabling was provided for six horses.

The annual value was £30. However, three years later, the Gleaners status was increased to that of an alehouse and now was able to serve spirits, in addition to beer. The annual value rose to £80. In 1885 the then owner, Thomas

3.6 Gleaners 1998

Fletcher of Calverton sold the inn to William Henry Hutchinson, brewer of Basford - the Home Brewery by 1903. William Wibberley remained as the licensee until 1891. After succession of publicans [Table 10.], the Gleaners public house still exists in Calverton today owned by Scottish & Newcastle Breweries.

Gleaners were farm labourers, who gathered up ears of corn left by the reapers, and this would have been the inspiration for the naming of this public house. Their work was made famous by Jean François Millet `The Gleaners', painted in 1857 which shows three sturdy peasant women in sunlit fields. It hangs in the Musée d'Orsay, in Paris. There was at one time, a Gleaners Arms in Talke near Stoke-on-Trent, but this has now been demolished.

Table 10.

Licensees of the Gleaners in Calverton

Period	Licensee	Period	Licensee
c.1835 to c.1860	John Collyer	1902 to 1908	Joseph Taylor
c.1860 to c.1872	William Cummins	1908 to 1912	Mary Ann Taylor
c.1872 to 1891	William Wibberley	1912 to 1944	Richard Brown
1891 to c.1894	Thomas Taylor Fletcher	1944 to 1958	Richard Cooper
1894 to 1896	Henry Middup	1958 to 1964	Charles Peter Smart
1896 to1897	Thomas Clare Kirk	1964 to 1985	Frederick Kendall Squires
1897 to 1899	Richard Gibson	1985 to 1986	Carl Desmond Staton
1899 to 1902	John Henshaw	1986 to 2005	Eric Hurst

In the nineteenth century the Gleaners had a club room which was of sufficient size to accommodate large meetings.

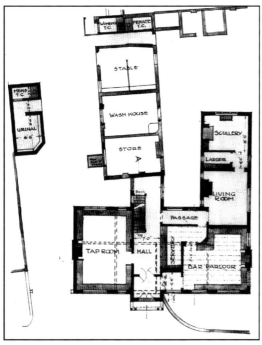

Plan 4 Ground Floor of the Gleaners dated 20th April 1923

*On Wednesday the 6th January 1847, the members and friends of the Thornywood Lodge held their annual ball and tea-party, at **Collyer's** the **sign of the Gleaner**, when one hundred and twenty partook of the cup which refreshes, but does not inebriate. After tea, dancing commenced and was kept up till morning[16].*

It has been noted that at least one coroner's inquest was held here although the majority of these, in Calverton, were held at either the Admiral Rodney or the White Lion.

Inquest on a Child: *An inquest was held on the 1st of March 1858, at the Gleaner public house, Calverton, on the body of Francis William Cund, an infant, seven months old, the son of Thomas Cund, a framework knitter. He had been ill at times, since birth, but during the last fortnight, had suffered from a discharge of blood from the nose in the mornings and more recently his throat was swollen. Late on Friday evening the child suddenly died in the arms of his mother. At the inquest it transpired that, about a fortnight previous, two girls, the child's sisters, when carrying a rabbit to a neighbour's house, quarrelled as to who should hold the child and he was accidentally dropped onto the ground, hitting its head. Verdict: Accidental death, but accelerated by a fall.*

This club room still survived in 1923 and was located on the first floor. The ground floor plan of 1923 [Plan 4. page 17.] shows that the Gleaners had three public areas and the stables with two stalls still existed; originally there were four. In 1996 an extension to the lounge bar was carried out by Scottish & Newcastle Breweries but they ensured that the alterations preserved the well-established image of the public house, as a traditional local. The lounge bar was given a totally new-look interior including a new bar and fittings, complete redecoration, new carpeting and soft furnishing. The licensee at the time, Eric Hirst, was confident that the Gleaners would attract more people for bar snacks whilst still maintaining its reputation as a traditional local public house.

Frederick Kendall Squires held the Licence for the Gleaners from 1964 until 1985. He was originally a bookbinder for Boots the Chemists prior to entering the public house trade. The accompanying photograph shows him on the steps of the Gleaners with his faithful dog, Rocky.

3.7 Frederick K. Squires c.1975

Hutt

This inn stood near to a small lake, known as Archer's Water, on the Dover Beck on the edge of the parish of Calverton. Traditionally it had a dreadful reputation. This ill-reputed inn was sited nearby the drovers' road, over which cattle were driven from Scotland. Reminiscences claim that many a poor Highlander lies in the boggy lake or in one of the quiet lanes surreptitiously abstracted from his cattle and helped out of the world by a villainous contrivance of landlord and landlady of the Hutt. However, all these misdemeanours apparently took place many years before 1780 when Abraham Wood was the innkeeper and his forename became associated with the Hutt. There are a limited number of references to this property which is shown on the Calverton Enclosure map of 1780 [Figure 3.8 page 19] as being on a piece of land of six acres and one rood on the edge of the parish. The previous year a meeting of the arbitrators, for setting the position of the boundary between the parishes of Calverton and Blidworth, was held at Abraham's Hutt. The following day, a second meeting was held at the house of William Redgate in Calverton [the White Lion], to proceed with the execution of the Enclosure. A number of deeds have survived between 1780, and 1788 which relate to changes in ownership and those renting the Hutt.

An indenture dated 7ᵗʰ July 1780 *refers to Abraham Wood, innkeeper, of the Hutt in the parish of Calverton and Elizabeth his wife on the one part and Thomas Higgins of Mansfield. It refers to land in the Forest of Sherwood whereon a dwelling house stands called the Hutt containing six acres and one rood which was granted to Thomas Higgins*[17].

Abraham Wood died in 1785 and is buried at Calverton; subsequent to his death a James Archer was associated with the Hutt. His occupation was given as a rabbit seller living in Nottingham; he was possibly related to Archer whose name is associated with the small lake on the Dover Beck. An inventory of James Archers' goods to the value of

£63-0s.-11d., was recorded in January1788[18]. Two months later Margaret Sherbrooke of Oxton acquired the Hutt, or at least use of it, and it seems very likely that at this time it ceased to be used as a public house[19]. It is however, interesting to note that a farm called Archer's Water Farm, currently stands close to the Old Rufford Road [the A614], near to the site of Archer's Water and the site of the Hutt public house.

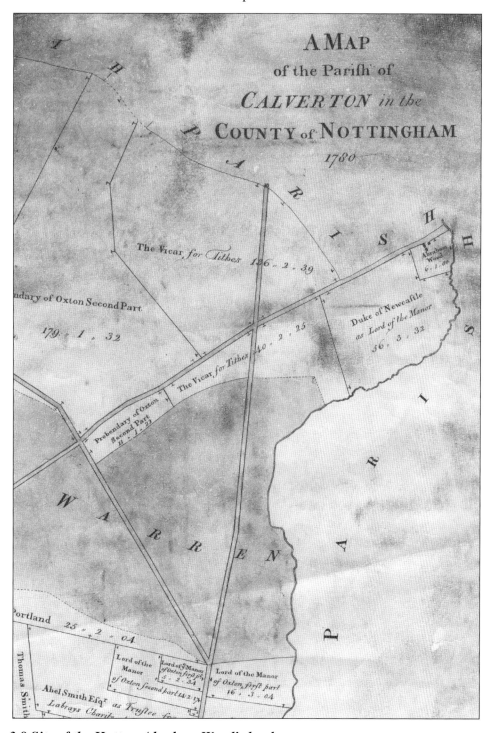

3.8 Site of the Hutt on Abraham Wood's land

Queen's Head

First recorded in 1759 and the last record was in 1773 when the inn-keeper was William Baguley. In 1764 a George Castle was recorded as being a victualler in Calverton and he may possibly have been a tenant of the Queen's Head.

To be sold by auction: *At the Queen's Head in Calverton five miles from Nottingham in the Forest, upon Monday and Tuesday the 8th and 9th days of October 1759 beginning at eleven o'clock each day in the morning,* [a number of closes of land are listed][20].

To be sold by auction: *On Tuesday the 23ʳᵈ day of February 1773, at the house of Wm. Baguley, being the Sign of the Queen's Head, in Calverton in the County of Nottingham between the hours of two and four in the afternoon.* [Two tenements, outbuildings, gardens and land are listed.][21] The site of the Queen's is not known but is possible that some time between 1773 and 1783 it was re-named the Admiral Rodney.

White Lion

First recorded in the local newspapers in 1773 but almost certainly may have existed earlier, at that time; the other hostelry in the village was the Queen's Head. William Redgate was the alehouse keeper in this year and he remained in charge of the White Lion for another 20 years. His successor, William Mitchell, was convicted along with Thomas Wood of the Admiral Rodney for allowing drinking during the period of divine service on a Sunday [see above]. During the late 1790's the recently formed local Friendly Society met at the White Lion. Mitchell only appears to have remained a licensee for a few years, although those that followed tended to keep the public house for long periods and on the death of the publican it was common practice for his widow to assume to the licence. The White Lion has always been a fully-licensed house and in 1872, was described as having two parlours, a bar, tap-room

3.9 White Lion 1998

and a club-room and stabling for 5 horses. It also sat in 14 acres of land and its annual value was £84. A solicitor, a Mr. William Williams owned it, but later it was sold to the Fletcher family, who also owned the Gleaners and were tenants of the White Lion. In 1887, the ownership passed to the Brewer, William Henry Hutchinson and so joined the Gleaners that had been sold to the same Company two years earlier. As with many public houses, extensive modifications and alterations to the fabric of the building took place during the next century. In 2010 a major renovation of the White Lion was carried out. It then opened as a public house styled a Lounge & Restaurant and renamed Oscars.

The changes in the licensees are listed in Table 11. on page 21.

The site plan in 1959 shows the recently created car park for the White Lion and the proposed new roads in Calverton.

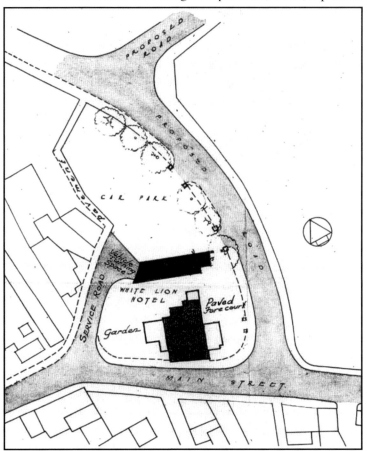

3.10 White Lion site plan 1959

Calverton Inclosure: *The Proprietors of the open and common field, and such as are entitled to common right, within the parish of Calverton, in the County of Nottingham, are desired to meet on Tuesday the 7ᵗʰ day of December 1773 at the house of Mr. Wm. Redgate, known by the sign of the White Lyon, in Calverton; to confider whether it will be proper to apply to the next sessions of Parliament, for an Act, to inclose the open fields and commons within the said parish[22].*

Table 11.

Licensees of the White Lion in Calverton

Period	Licensee	Period	Licensee
c.1773 to c.1797	William Redgate	c.1956 to c.1965	Frank Hall
c.1797 to c.1799	William Mitchell	c.1965 to 1967	Frank Barnes
c.1809 to 1811	Mr. Wilson	1967 to 1974	Thomas George Church
c.1811 to c.1829	Joseph Brunt	1974 to 1986	Robert Tull Griffiths
c.1829 to 1878	Samuel Fletcher	1986 to 1989	Barry Leslie Willett
1878 to 1886	Catherine Fletcher	1989 to 1991	Anthony James Berry
1886 to 1887	Ester Ann Fletcher	1991 to 1993	Peter Briggs
1887 to 1892	Nicholas Lee	1993 to 1998 (06)	Deana Claire Louise Bettison
1892 to 1893	Clara Lee		& James William Twells
1893 to 1905	John Robinson	1998 (06) to 1998 (11)	Stephen Edward Miller
1905 to 1915	Clara Robinson	1998 (11) to 1999	Mark Edwin Lamb
1915 to 1917	Eliza Tilley	1999 to 2000	Keith Lacey
1917 to 1918	George Thomas Hague	2000 to 2001	Lisa Tynan
1918 to 1940	William Coxon	2001 to 2003	Nicholas Martin Johnson
1940 to c.1956	William James Gurton Hall	2003 to	Kevin & Akile Addison

Over the years many auctions of property, land etc. were held in the White Lion, e.g. in 1797[23] and in 1831 a chapel was sold in Calverton[24], and the White Lion was advertised for rent in 1832[25]. Between 1835 and 1865, 15 coroners' inquests were held (Miscellany Table 1.]. One is summarised below

An inquest was held on Monday the 19th May 1845 at the house of Mr. Samuel Fletcher, the sign of the White Lion, Calverton, to ascertain the cause of death of Joseph Kirkham. The deceased was a framework knitter, a bachelor, 33 years old, residing at Woodborough and lodged at the house of William Forman, a relative. Eleven weeks ago he had a pain in his face and had three or four teeth drawn. Being no better he took a large quantity of mercury, which produced a high state of salivation, which combined with a disease of the lungs bid defiance to medical skill and caused his death. Verdict: That the diseased has died a natural death from disease of the lungs, but that his death was accelerated by the effects of mercury, which he had taken, but no evidence appears to prove by whom the mercury was administrated.

Unnamed Beer-shops

Subsequent to the Beer Act of 1830 three Beer-shops opened in Calverton. Although to date it has not been possible to ascertain whether these outlets carried a name, according to the 1832 Trade Directory they were under the control of Lot Smith, Samuel Taylor and Ann Watts. This class of premises has been recorded up to 1865; one may have been the precursor of the Forest Tavern.

4. CAYTHORPE

During the seventeenth century two alehouse keepers have been noted. In 1619/20 John Mafield, a victualler of Cathorpe, [the earlier name for Caythorpe] was convicted for allowing unlawful games in his alehouse and was committed to gaol, but later released. Richard Thornhill was indicted for brewing in 1640 without having obtained a licence and fined 6d. Although it would be surprising if an alehouse did not exist in this village during the next century, we have to wait until the surviving records list the Volunteer in 1811.

Black Horse

This building most certainly is very old but it is unclear when it became a public house. It does not feature in the Alehouse Recognizances which have survived from 1809 to 1826, nor is it listed in the 1832 or 1844 trade directories. There appears to be a building or a group of cottages on the site of the Black Horse on the 1766 enclosure map

4.1 Sketch of Black Horse 1957

of Caythorpe/Lowdham but whether this was an alehouse is pure conjecture. The first reference I have found to the Black Horse, as a licensed public house, was in the Nottingham Review of the 29th August 1851[26]. However it may well have succeeded one of Caythorpe's beer-shops established after 1830. The most likely contender would be that initially run by the Tomlinson family for this was of sufficient size to accommodate coroners' inquests [see below]. However, by 1851 this establishment had closed its doors.

There is an oft reported anecdote that a highwayman, going by the name of Dick Turpin, sometimes stayed at an alehouse in Caythorpe, which is said to have been the Black Horse. The number of public houses claiming that Dick Turpin stayed at or visited their premises is legion and only in a very few instances can it be substantiated[27]. One hundred years after Turpin's death, William Harrison Ainsworth published a romantic best-selling novel, "Rookwood" in which he portrays Turpin as a courageous, dare-devil figure, elegantly dressed and handsome, robbing the rich[28]. In reality Richard [Dick] Turpin, the son of John and Mary Turpin, born in Essex in 1705, a butcher by trade, drifted into violent gang-crime. This early part of his life is well-documented; he was part of a gang of criminals [the Essex gang] who targeted country houses, violently attacking the occupants, until they revealed where they had hidden their money and valuables; they then took their booty back to London. Some of the gang were eventually caught but Turpin was lucky to escape, and he subsequently became a highwayman, but he too was later apprehended and hanged at York in 1739[27]. A few years after Ainsworth's novel of 1834 and the changed perception of Turpin, in the public eye it is feasible to suggest that the first landlord of the Black Horse, Francis Ekring, named the public house in memory of Turpin's fictitious horse, *"Black Bess"*. Although he appears to have had no documentary evidence, he may also have started a rumour that Turpin visited Caythorpe over a hundred years ago. The only written evidence I have found of the Caythorpe connection was in a pamphlet, written in 1924 by Louis Mellard[29]. He said that he was quoting from a diary [he claimed that it was now lost], and had been written by a Lincolnshire farmer. However, on a letter of 1955[30], by K.T. Hartlett, Editor-in-chief, of the Guardian Journal, he wrote in script, that Mellards' reminiscences were tarradiddle. It appears that Mellard later admitted, that his story

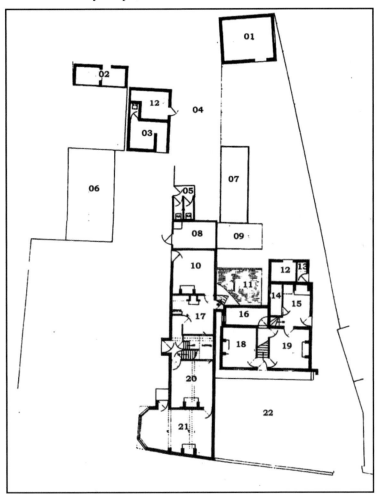

Plan 5 Ground Floor of the Black Horse 23rd May 1946
01= Cow Shed; 02= Piggery; 03= Gents; 04= Skittle Alley;
05= Ladies; 06= Shelter; 07= Shed; 08= Wash House;
09= Garage; 10= Living Rm.; 11= Cellar Under; 12= Store;
13= Toilet; 14 & 16= Pantry; 15= Kitchen; 17= Best Rm.;
18= Sitting Rm.; 19= Living Rm.; 20= Tap Rm.; 21= Vaults
22= Garden

was fictitious, but that there was a grain of truth here and there. However, whatever the truth, it is a nice story to relate and so is that of Robin Hood. The fame of Turpin is universally well-known; over the years there have been very many plays, books, pamphlets, children's stories written not only in this country but overseas. He even features in the carry-on series of films on television `Carry on Dick'.

4.2 The Lounge of the Black Horse 1957

The first licensee of the Black Horse was Francis Ekring. Although Ekring was summoned before the magistrates in 1856 for a breach of the Licensed Victuallers Act, [usually: allowing drunkenness, opening during divine service on Sundays, using unjust measures, keeping a disorderly house or allowing gambling on his premises] for this crime he received a warning but his Licence was not disallowed[31]. By 1872, Robert Branson, a hosier of Caythorpe owned the Black Horse. After Robert's death his widow, Ann Branson was, in 1881, the recorded owner until James Shipstone & Sons Ltd., Brewers, Basford acquired the Black Horse in 1894. However, the Branson family continued to have an interest in the public house, for Richard Branson was the licensee from 1st July 1893 until 1st July 1905 and other members were tenants until John Frederick Sherwin took over from the late Florence Branson on 8th March 1955. The Black Horse has continued for over 30 years under the stewardship of two ladies, Pauline Margery Andrews, from 12th March 1970 and her daughter, Sharron Diona Andrews, from 15th October 1986 to the present day. In past years it has been the haunt of many famous Nottinghamshire cricketers; great names and personalities like William Gunn, Wilfred Flowers and Mordecai Sherwin were frequent visitors. Mr. Sherwin a one time landlord was the grandson of the latter mentioned cricketer. The Black Horse is now a free house owned by Sharron Andrews. The list of licensees is recorded in Table 12.

Table 12.

Licensees of the Black Horse in Caythorpe

Period	Licensee	Period	Licensee
c.1851 to c.1861	Francis Ekring	1893 to 1905	Richard Branson
c.1861 to c.1869	George Kirk	1905 to 1913	Elizabeth Branson
c.1869 to c. 1872	Richard Bullers	1913 to 1927	Richard Alexis Branson
c.1872 to 1874	George Bailey	1927 to 1955	Florence Mary Branson
1874 to 1877	Frederick Swinson	1955 to 1969	John Frederick Sherwin
1877 to 1887	George Burrows	1969 to 1970	Dennis Burrows
1887 to 1888	George Oxley	1970 to 1986	Pauline Margery Andrews
1888 to 1893	John Towle	1986 to	Sharron Diona Andrews

Two coroners' inquests, in 1851 and 1854, have been recorded at the Black Horse [Miscellany Table 1.]. A précis of one of these is given below and is as stated above the first mention of the Black Horse.

Child Poisoning with Narcotics: *On Tuesday 26th August 1851, an inquest was held before Mr. Coroner Swann at the Black Horse public house, Caythorpe, on the body of Samuel Thompson aged 15 weeks, the son of Joseph Thompson, framework knitter, of that place. From the evidence of a woman named Ann Edwards, it seems the child had been very poorly for two or three weeks, and on Saturday night he became convulsed. Early on the following morning a dose of Godfrey's cordial and syrup of rhubarb was administered to him and another at six o'clock in the evening. Shortly afterwards he was again seized with a convulsive fit, in which he died. Verdict, Natural death but that its death was accelerated by doses of a certain mixture of Godfrey's cordial and syrup of rhubarb.*

Old Volunteer [formally the Volunteer]

4.3 Old Volunteer 1997

First recorded in the Alehouses Recognizances of 1811[32] and in a newspaper advertisement in 1815[33], but the Volunteer may have been in existence a few years earlier. At this time Richard Wilson held the licence, he was 43, and eleven years later in May 1822 he married Hannah Chantry of the same parish. Although Richard signed the marriage register, Hannah appended her mark. Unfortunately in August of the following year he died and was buried at Lowdham on the 7th

I Samuel Oldacre the minister of the Township of Caythorpe in the County of Nottingham do sincerely certify that Hannah Wilson the widow of Richard Wilson of the said Township has not kept a public house in the said parish that her said husband was licensed at the last general licensing day to keep a common ale or public house called the Volunteer in the said Township and lately departed this life and the said Hannah Wilson is now residing in the said public house and is a person of good fame and of sober life and conversation worthy to be entrusted with the licence to keep in the house a victualling house in the said Township of Caythorpe.

Dated this 14th September 1823.

Samuel Oldacre Curate

4.4 Transcript of a letter from Samuel Oldacre

of the month aged 54 years. His new wife succeeded to the licence of the Volunteer. However, it was necessary, as a new licensee, for her to first obtain a certificate of good conduct from the local vicar [see the transcript of a letter from Samuel Oldacre in Figure 4.4.]. A facsimile of her alehouse licence is reproduced on page vi Figure 0.1. In 1826 Hannah had a son Henry Hardy but sadly the following year both mother and son had passed away and the Volunteer came under the control of Henry Paling a member of a local family. There were two recorded owners of the Volunteer, James Sears, cottager from Lowdham and Arthur Gunn, a publican from Bulwell; he later also became the tenant. However, when Gunn left the Volunteer on the 25th August 1897 it was sold to Hardy Kimberley Ltd., Brewers of Kimberley. In 2009 this inn, under new ownership, was extensively modernised.

Table 13.
Licensees of the Old Volunteer in Caythorpe

Period	Licensee	Period	Licensee
c.1811 to 1823	Richard Wilson	1915 to 1916	George Henry Skinner
1823 to c.1827	Hannah Wilson	1916 to 1930	Samuel Hysop
c.1827 to c.1861	Henry Paling	1930 to 1937	Ernest Edward Willment
c.1861 to c.1864	William Challand	1937 to 1947	Thomas Henry Taylor
c.1864 to c.1869	Samuel Martin	1947 to 1950	Arthur Cooling Beeley
c.1869 to 1878	John Sears	1950 to 1954	Edward Robinson Hardy
1878 to 1883	William Allen	1954 to 1955	Katherine Vesta Wesley-Roads
1883 to 1886	Mary Allen	1955 to 1964	Lancelot Frederick Green
1886 to 1887	Frederick Key	1964 to 1975	William Henry Dennis
1887 to 1889	William Suffolk	1975 to 1983	Kenneth Hill
1889 to 1891	John Thomas Leivers	1983 to 1989	Pauline Mitchell
1891 to 1897	Arthur Gunn	1989 to 1996	Michael Adams
1897 to 1898 (03)	James Hawkins	1996 to 1999	Susan Jane Stirland
1898 (03) to 1898 (09)	Lawrence Cyrus Boot	1999 to 2000	Christine Mavis Day
1898 (09) to 1901	Herbert Collinwood Merryweather	2000 to 2003	Joanne Louise Conners
1901 to 1907	George Oldershaw	2003 to 2004	Gillian Scott
1907 to 1908	Henry Marson	2004 to 2005	Deborah Angela Ferris
1908 to 1915	Clara Jane Marson	2005 to	Deborah Angela Ferris & Ian Joseph Ferris

Six coroners' inquests were held at the Volunteer between 1830 and 1865 [Miscellany Table 1.]. One is illustrated below.

Death from Drowning: *An inquest was held on Tuesday the 4th March 1845 at the house of Henry Paling, the sign of the Volunteer at Caythorpe on view the body of Edward Thomas Wain, six years old. The deceased was the son of Charles Wain of Caythorpe, framework-knitter, and on Monday morning was sent, between nine and ten o'clock, to Lowdham, with his sister, aged eight years, to fetch some bread. Whilst on the way, the deceased jumped upon some drifted snow by the side of a dyke and accidentally fell in and was drowned. The dyke was about half full of water and the current strong and rapid. The little girl was afraid to go into the water to fetch her little brother out, for fear that she would also be drowned; she screamed and ran for assistance. The ostler at the Magna Charta public house overheard her, and ran and got the child out of the water, but life was extinct. Verdict: Accidentally drowned.*

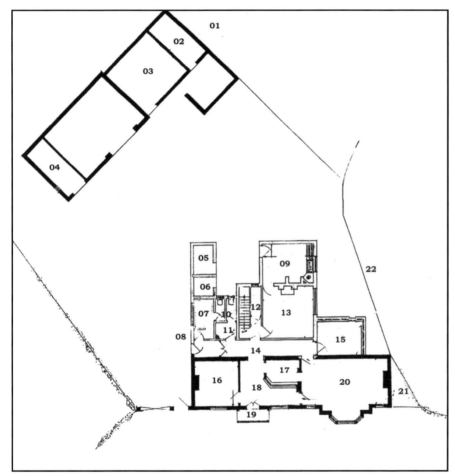

The plan in the accompanying figure shows the ground floor of the Volunteer after the extensions to the building were carried out about November 1936. The original washhouse was demolished and a new kitchen, bottle store, coal-house and interior urinal built. In addition a new side-door to the garden and an internal corridor was added. The original plans do not show a club room but it may have been the area later used as a wash house or possibly it was on the first floor, but by 1936 it had been converted into extra bedrooms.

Plan 6 Ground Floor of the Volunteer dated November 1936
01= Garden; 02= Store; 03= Stable; 04= Barn; 05= Bottle Store; 06= Coals; 07= Urinal; 08= Garden Entrance; 09= Kitchen; 10= WC's; 11= Ladies; 12= Larder 13= Living Room; 14= Passage; 15= Beer Cellar; 16= Tap Room; 17= Servery; 18= Hall; 19= Porch; 20= Lounge; 21= Old Urinal Removed; 22= Stream

Unnamed Beer-shops

A number of persons have been associated with the above class of premises in Caythorpe between 1832 and 1849. Those ran by William Jerram, Samuel Hardy and James Pearce were probably small cottages or farms. It has been suggested that the sites of these may have been at Brook Cottage, Red Tag Cottage, Manor Farm and Ivy Cottage at various times[34]. As previously stated, another beer-shop, initially controlled by the Tomlinson family was sufficiently large to accommodate coroners' inquests and it seems feasible that it was the precursor to the Black Horse. Prior to holding the tenancy of this beer-shop John Tomlinson was a butcher in Caythorpe but it appears that about 1847 he relinquished control of his beer-shop in favour of his son Samuel. However this was short-lived and another butcher in Caythorpe, Arthur Allcock took over the tenancy but again this lasted for little over a year. On the 26th June 1849 the premises were auctioned at the Magna Charta Inn, in Lowdham[35]. From the published schedule we see that they were reasonably large.

To be sold by auction: *at the house of Mr Jamson, the Magna Charta Inn, in Lowdham, in the county of Nottingham, on Tuesday the 26th June 1849, at three o'clock in the afternoon, a number of lots of land and houses in Caythorpe and Hoveringham.*
Lot 5: All that Retail Beerhouse [Retail Beer-Shop], with stables, outbuildings and gardens situate in Caythorpe, now in the occupation of Joseph Allcock, containing an area of 1,440 square yards.

Table 14.

Tenants of an unnamed beer-shop [possibly re-named the Black Horse c.1849] in Caythorpe

Period	Tenant
c.1841 to c.1847	John Tomlinson
c.1847 to c.1848	Samuel Tomlinson
c.1848 to c.1849	Arthur Allcock

In the month, following the above auction Arthur Allcock was convicted of stealing two cows and for this crime he was sent to prison[36], and undoubtedly his time at the Caythorpe beer-shop came to an end and I suggest that the new owners re-named it the Black Horse and successfully obtained an alehouse licence. Shortly before this auction, John Tomlinson died and at the time of the 1851 census his wife Elizabeth and his son, Richard, were living elsewhere in Caythorpe, whilst the elder son, Samuel, was a farmer of 25 acres in the village.

In July 1849 Arthur Allcock, butcher and beerhouse keeper, of Caythorpe, aged 54, was arraigned on the charge of stealing two heifers, at parish of Burton Joyce on the 18th of May, the property of Melicent Hardy. The chairman summed up in a masterly and elaborate manner and the jury returned a verdict of guilty, with a recommendation to mercy on account of previous good conduct. Allcock was sentenced to six months hard labour in Southwell house of correction with four weeks in a solitary cell.

Three coroners' inquests were held at Tomlinson's retail beerhouse between 1845 and 1847 [Miscellany Table 1.]. One of these referred to a young woman who took her own life and is annotated below,

Suicide by a Female: *On Thursday the 7th January 1847, C. Swann Esq. held an inquest at Mr. Samuel Tomlinson's retail beerhouse in Caythorpe, upon Mary Ann Tomlinson. Deceased was a single woman, 25 years old and daughter of John Tomlinson of the above village. He stated that in the months of September and October last year, his daughter had typhus fever from which she recovered but that her intellects became impaired. About five weeks ago he discovered her up stairs with a knife across her throat which she appeared to be going to cut but he took the knife from her. He then related other acts of the deceased, which showed that she had a strong tendency to commit suicide. In the afternoon of Tuesday prior to the inquest she got out of the house and was proceeding to the River Trent, as it was supposed, to drown herself, but a neighbour brought her back. In the night of the same day, she got out of bed, procured a table knife and cut her throat in her chamber. Her father and relatives were ignorant of the melancholy circumstance until after eight o'clock the following morning when her father found her quite dead, cold and stiff. A table knife, covered with blood, lay under her breast and she had completely severed either the left carotid or jugular vein. The father said that he had another daughter whose intellect had been weak for years. He imputed blame to the overseers for not taking his daughter [the deceased] to the Asylum, having made an application for that purpose. However, after a lengthy statement by John Tomlinson, the jury were unanimously of the opinion that no blame was attached to the parish authorities and returned the following verdict: That the deceased died in consequence of cutting her throat, she being of unsound mind at the time.*

It is not clear whether or not John Tomlinson and his family were still living at this retail beerhouse where this melancholy event took place.

5. EPPERSTONE

The first alehouse recorded in Epperstone, was in 1604, when in April of that year, William Ward was indicted for not having a licence to brew ale. Later, members of the Ricket family were also prosecuted for brewing illegally and for entertaining during divine service. Mrs. Statham, a widow, was censured for allowing drinking at night in her alehouse. During the next century two inns were noted, the King's Head and the Marquis of Granby. In addition there are a number of newspaper references between 1761 and 1773 to sales of trees and estates at the house of Elizabeth Dufty in Epperstone. It is open to conjecture whether or not these took place on licensed premises.

Cross Keys

This public house existed in Epperstone from 1811[37] or possibly earlier, it may have originally been called the Marquis of Granby noted in a newspaper advertisement dated 1785. In 1872 the Cross Keys was owned by Robert Holden of Nuthall and later transferred to the Reverend James Richard Holden of Bury St. Edmunds. By 1883 it had been purchased by Frederick Hucknall, a farmer residing in Lowdham. The Cross Keys appears to have remained in private hands until at least 1945 and some time later it was purchased by the Hardy Hanson, Kimberley Brewery. In the 1870's the Cross Keys had nine rooms, four of which were open to the public, its stables could accommodate four horses and had 20 acres of land. The annual value was £54. Although I have not found a plan for the interior of the Cross Keys, from the

5.1 Sketch of the Cross Keys c. 1950

foregoing it appears to be fairly spacious. It was able to accommodate various local meetings, the Back Lodge Order of Odd Fellows routinely met here; their Lodge room was in this public house[38]. It is believed that in 1860 a volunteer rifle company known as the Thorneywood Chase Corps was formed here. This inn remains in the village at the time of writing, a list of licensees is given in Table 15.

Timber: *To be sold by private contract in one or more lots upwards of one thousand oak, ash and elm trees, standing, marked and numbered, at a place called Bosin Wood, in the parish of Epperstone and County of Nottingham. – Mr. Sardesson, on the premises will show the trees. The sale will be on Friday the 13th 1785 at the sign of the Marquis of Granby, in Epperstone, aforesaid, at ten o'clock in the forenoon*[39].

Table 15.

Licensees of the Cross Keys in Epperstone

Period	Licensee	Period	Licensee
c.1811 to c.1824	Thomas Harrison	1888 to 1891	Anne Knight (widow)
c.1824 to c.1834	Robert Hopkinson	1891 to 1904	Anne Foster (late Anne Knight)
c.1834 to c.1841	Gervas Martin	1904 to 1911	Harry Birkin
c.1841 to c.1843	John Leafe	1911 to 1925	George Brooker
c.1843 to c.1847	George Kemp	1925 to 1945	James Tuxford
c.1847 to c.1851	Thomas Towers	1945 to 1967	Donald Robert Girling Crisp
c.1851 to c.1871	John Wheatley		& Margaret Norah Crisp
c.1871 to 1880	Edwin Sampson	1967 to 1969	Joseph Richard Teatum
1880 to 1881 (02)	John Needham	1969(02) to 1976	Joseph Frank Davies
1881 (02) to 1881 (05)	Thomas Burrows	1976 to 1984	John E. Butcher
1881 (05) to 1883	John Lamin	1984 to 1998	Barry Taylor
1883 to 1888	Edwin Knight	1998 to 2002	David Arthur Rose
		2002 to	Alan Thompson

Thirteen coroners' inquests were held at the Cross Keys between 1829 and 1854 (Miscellany Table 1.) and one is summarized below.

Suicide by Hanging: *An inquest was held on Saturday the 18ᵗʰ April 1829 at the house of Robert Hopkinson, the Cross Keys, Epperstone, on view of the body of William Adkin. The deceased had been unwell for some time and the family have had the fever in their house for the last two months. Apparently Adkin went missing from his house and two witnesses went to look for him and he was eventually found in a plantation called Epperstone or Adkin's Dumble. He was hanging upon a bough of a tree and both his feet rested on the slope of a bank. There was a cord [a piece of plough-line] in a draw noose around his neck and the other end of the cord was fastened to the bough of the tree. He was quite dead and appeared to have been hanging about two days. It seems that a number of family relatives have been deranged and an aunt had destroyed herself in a similar way. Verdict: Hung himself, being at the time in an unsound state of mind.*

King's Head

Situated in the Main Street, further along from the Cross Keys, the building is now a private house. It was first recorded in 1783, in an advertisement from the Nottingham Journal offering this public house for sale[40]. At that time it was

5.2 King's Head c.1908

in the possession of a Mrs. Worthington, so it is clear that the King's Head must have been established at an earlier date. In 1813, William Epperson acquired the tenancy[41], and he remained at the King's Head until his death on 23ʳᵈ February 1839 and from his obituary it appears that he was a popular and much respected landlord[42]. However, the ownership of this public house remained with the Epperson family until 1874 when it was acquired by an estate agent from Nottingham, Thomas Huskinson. At that time the King's Head had eight rooms; three of them open to the public, and stabling for six horses with an annual value of £13. After further changes in private ownership the inn was sold to Hansons, Brewer of Kimberley in 1899. In 1917, the licensing authorities came to the conclusion that one public house was sufficient, for the needs of the village, and the following year the licence for the King's Head was not renewed. On the 30ᵗʰ March 1918 it closed its doors[43].

To be sold: *and entered upon immediately a good public house, known by the Sign of the King's Head, now in possession of Mrs Worthington; with outhouses, yard, and good garden and brewing vessels, situate at Epperstone, in the County of Nottingham. For further particulars enquire of Mr. George Briggs, of Epperstone, aforesaid.* [December 1783]

Table 16.

Licensees of the King's Head in Epperstone

Period	Licensee	Period	Licensee
c.1783 and earlier	Mrs. Worthington (owner)	1898 to 1901	Francis Luckett
c.1813 to c.1839	William Epperson	1901 to 1904	Albert Joseph Pearce
c.1839 to c.1843	Robert Epperson	1904 to 1905	James Frederick Mason
c.1843 to c.1861	Sarah Cutts	1905 to 1916	Thomas Thornhill
c.1861 to 1896	William Skinner	1916 to 1917	Josiah Shepherd
1896 to 1898	Thomas Daybell	1917 to 1918	Elizabeth Shepherd

There were two coroners' inquests held at the King's Head in 1864 and 1865 (Miscellany Table 1.). One of these is summarised below.

Death of a child: *Mr. H. Swann, deputy coroner, held an inquest on Tuesday 23rd February 1864 at the King's Head, Epperstone, on the body of Mary Editha, illegitimate daughter of Charlotte Harrison, single woman. The child was three months old and had suffered some days from a cold. The mother took it to bed with her a little before midnight on Saturday and gave it food once during the night and at half-past seven the next morning found it dead beside her. The evidence of Mr. J. H. Osborne, surgeon, was to the fact that the child died from convulsions, caused by congestion of the lungs; and verdict to that effect was returned.*

Unnamed Beer-shop

There was one beer-shop that retailed beer for over 20 years [c.1832 to c.1856]; at the time of writing its location in Epperstone, has not been determined. It was under the sole control of William Foster, who opened his house under the terms of the Beer Act of 1830. This probably closed on the death of Foster in 1856, aged 77 years. He was buried in Epperstone on 4th November of that year, his wife Jane had pre-deceased him, dying in 1848, aged 72 years.

6. GONALSTON

In 1612/13 a warrant was issued for Robert Moreland, a baker, to answer a charge of brewing without having first obtained a licence, for keeping a disorderly house and for harbouring vagrants. He was again indicted the following year, for his failure to apply for a licence to brew ale. In 1630, two victuallers in Gonalston, William Clarke and Gilbert Swanwick, were prosecuted for selling ale above the statuary price. There is one reference in the next century to a public house in Gunnerston [an earlier name for Gonalston] called the Fox & Crown[44]. This was noted in the Nottingham Journal of 1781 and refers to the sale of land. The site of this public house in the village is not known but the building must have been of reasonable size to accommodate an auction. No further references to licensed premises were seen in Gonalston during the 19th or 20th centuries. There were three coroners' inquests held in Gonalston, between 1834 and 1845, but these were held in private houses, and this may suggest there were no suitable licensed houses at this time.

To be sold by auction: *or by private contract at the house of Thomas Barker's the Fox and Crown, in Gunnerston, in the County of Nottingham, on Friday, the 7th of September 1781, between the hours of three and six in the afternoon: A close of good freehold land, containing about fix acres, three roods, more or less, lying in the parish of Epperstone.*

7. GUNTHORPE

Undoubted there has been an alehouse in Gunthorpe, for very many years, associated with the ferry-crossing over the River Trent. The first indication comes in 1605/06, when Robert Oram was indicted for brewing and baking without a licence, and some time later, in 1614/15, Robert Orme [probably the same person] was again before the Court for a similar offence. In 1634, it is recorded that Henry Dawson, was prosecuted for harbouring vagrants, [although no occupation was given, he was probably a keeper of an alehouse], likewise in the following year, Robert Goodwin was indicted for brewing ale, without having first obtained a licence. In his will, dated 14th December 1694, and proved 19th January 1695, Thomas Marshall of Gunthorpe, was described as a husbandman, aleman and victualler. There are a number of references to innkeepers in Gunthorpe during, the 1700's, and it is surmised that they kept the Ferry or possibly the Anchor.

Anchor Inn

This Inn was first recorded in 1795 during the severe flooding that occurred in villages bordering the River Trent.

7.1 Anchor Inn 1997

At Gunthorpe: a small house to the right of the Anchor public house was actually immersed above the eaves[45]. However thirty years earlier on the enclosure map of Gunthorpe dated 1766 a building is shown on the site which approximates to the position of the present day Inn. In the early years of the next century, the licensee was Robert White[46], followed by William Huskinson in 1811. On the 31st March 1861, James Tomlinson publican of the Anchor, committed suicide by cutting his throat [see below]. His widow, Jane Tomlinson took over the Anchor public house until 1868, when in that year she married Samuel Rawson, who subsequently became the licensee. By 1872 the Anchor was owned by John Leland Oldacre

[gentleman] of Gunthorpe; it had stabling, a bar, tap room, parlour and clubroom. The annual value was £38. At this time, Samuel Rawson was the licensee and the following year he attempted to commit suicide by hanging himself and was fined 10s. 6d. [52½p.]. He had previously incurred a fine, of 21s. [£1.05p.], for allowing gambling to take place, within the Anchor public house. In the early years of the 19th century, the Anchor was the venue for visiting stallions to be mated, with local mares brought to the inn. The advertisements were voluminous extolling the pedigree and the virility of these horses. One such animal was brought to the Anchor in February 1813 the charges were three guineas and a crown for thorough-bred mare or two guineas and a crown for country mares. All demands to be paid at the time of covering or at mid-summer, mares proving barren last season half price[47].

After a succession of owners, the Anchor remained in private hands, until the Second World War [1939-45], when about this time it was sold to the Home Brewery. In 2009, the inn was re-furbished, and with a change in ownership and re-named the Pontifino, a restaurant, specialising in serving Italian food.

To be sold by auction: *by Mr. Gaskill at the house of Mr. Robert White, the sign of the Anchor in Gunthorpe, on Tuesday the 4th day of August 1801 at three o'clock in the afternoon, subject to such arrangements and conditions as will be produced at the time of sale: Lot 1. A cottage with outbuildings, yard and gardens, in the occupation of William Foster. Lot 2. A close called Bull-Piece, containing about 1 acre 3 roods and one Beast-gate in the common pasture equal to about 1 acre 2 roods. Lot 3. Fair Home Close containing about 1acre 1 rood and 14 perches. And one Beast-gate in the said pasture equal to about 1 acre 2 roods. Lots 2 and 3 are in the occupation of the said Robert White.*

Between 1838 and 1865 there were five coroners' inquests held at the Anchor [Miscellany Table 1.]. An extract of one is given below.

Suicide at Gunthorpe: *An inquest was opened on Tuesday the 2nd April 1861 at the Boat Inn [should read Anchor Inn], Gunthorpe, before Mr. Coroner Swann to inquire into the death of Mr. James Tomlinson, publican of that place, aged 45 years. It appears from the evidence of Jane Tomlinson, the deceased widow, that he got up on Sunday morning about five o'clock, leaving her in bed. He told her not to hurry about getting up as he would prepare breakfast. About half-past six she heard her son, Frederick screaming, and she immediately got up and went down stairs when she heard from him that the deceased had committed suicide in a stable adjoining the house. The instrument with which he effected his purpose was a hay-cutting knife and there was a deep wound on his throat. The deceased had been in a low state of mind for some time, but his wife was not apprehensive that he would commit suicide. The jury returned the following verdict: That the deceased cut his throat in a temporary fit of insanity.*

Table 17.

Licensees of the Anchor Inn in Gunthorpe

Period	Licensee	Period	Licensee
c.1795 to 1811	Robert White	1897 to 1900	Jennie Tomlinson
1811 to 1817	William Huskinson	1900 to 1902	William Arthur Barnes
1817 to 1820	William Wright	1902 to 1905	Benjamin Sadler
1820 to 1823	John Brittle	1905 to 1907	Harriet Osbourne
1823 to c.1832	Robert Stoakes	1907 to 1909	John Stockton
c.1832 to c.1841	Richard Attwood	1909 to 1911	Frank Atkinson
c.1841 to c.1855	Robert Knight	1911 to 1953	William Percy Day
c.1855 to 1861	James Tomlinson	1953 to 1958	John Desaguliers Newbury
1861 to 1868	Jane Tomlinson	1958 to 1964	George Montague Hall
1868 to 1876	Samuel Rawson	1964 to at least 1968	Eric Gordon Paling
1876 to 1882	Samuel Robinson	1989 (and earlier) to 1993	Jeremy Francis Scorer
1882 to 1885	Martha Robinson	1993 to 1996	Jeremy Francis &
1885 to 1897	Reubin Tomlinson		Amanda Margaret Scorer
		1996 to 1999	Jeremy Francis &
			Amanda Margaret Scorer &
			Richard Mark Bellamy
		1999 to 2008	Peter Dowling

Ferry/Unicorn

This public house almost certainly existed as an alehouse in the 1600's [see above]. However in the 18th century more definitive information is available and in 1716 the then controller of the ferry over the Trent, Mary Martin, was paid 10s. [50p.] for boating Dutch and Swiss solders over the river[48]. Nine years later, Maria Martin now described as a victualler, who has kept and maintained the ferry for many years, was indicted and fined 6d. [2½p.], for not keeping in good repair the rope, by which the ferryboat is hauled across the river. In the indictment, it was stated that it was the responsibility of the ferryman, [who was also the keeper of the nearby inn] from time immemorial, to maintain this rope, so enabling those persons and their horses to safely cross over the river Trent[49]. In

7.2 Unicorn 1997

the same year, she was also prosecuted for keeping a common and disorderly house. In 1736 Joseph Taylor succeeded to the tenancy. Mary Martin died in 1739 and her memorial stone survives in Lowdham graveyard. By 1820, the Ferry was usually called the Unicorn but for some years both names tended to be used. [It has been said that the name came from the Unicorn in Bulcote when it closed in 1864 but this clearly was not so.] In 1872, William Palmer who was at one time the landlord of the Wheat Sheaf in Sneinton owned the Unicorn. The Unicorn had facilities for stabling horses and the public rooms were: a bar, tap room, parlour and clubroom. The ground plan of 1927, for the Mansfield Brewery [Plan 7 page 32.], shows that the stables had survived, but the clubroom has not.

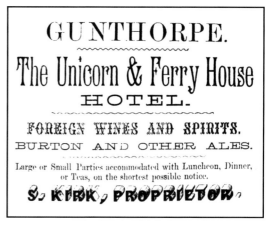

GUNTHORPE.

The Unicorn & Ferry House
HOTEL.

FOREIGN WINES AND SPIRITS.

BURTON AND OTHER ALES.

Large or Small Parties accommodated with Luncheon, Dinner, or Teas, on the shortest possible notice.

S. KIRK, PROPRIETOR.

7.3 Advertisement of 1869

It was probably on the first floor and by now converted to bedrooms. The annual value was £80 that included 8 acres of land. In 1900 Redgate Ltd., Wine & Spirit Merchants in Nottingham acquired the Unicorn but by 1919 it was again in private hands and remained so for many years until it again came under Brewery control. The plan of 1927 indicates that greater emphasis was being placed on the requirements of the travelling public. However, as far back as 1869 Samuel Kirk was promoting the Unicorn as a hotel. Today the Unicorn Hotel has been very much altered and enlarged and has sixteen en-suite bedrooms.

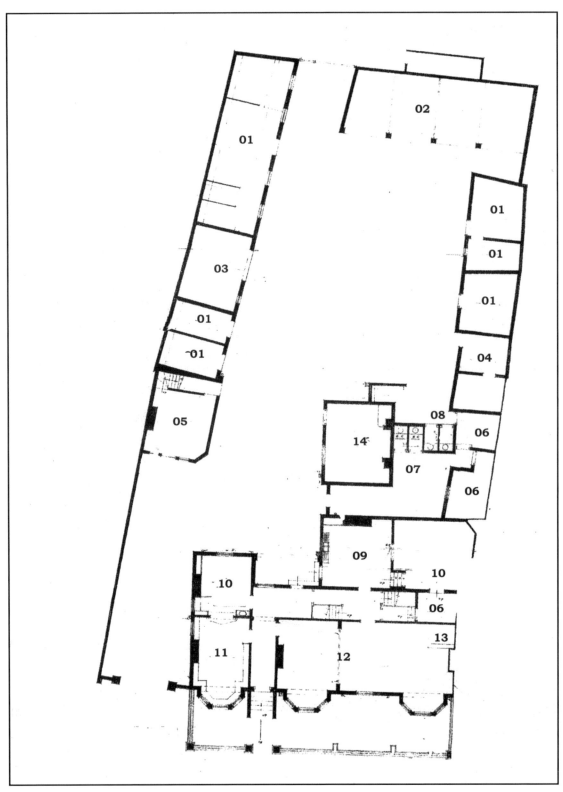

Plan 7 Ground Floor of the Unicorn dated December 1927
01= Stables; 02= Skittle Alley; 03= Garage; 04= Pig Sties; 05 & 06= Stores; 07= Ladies Toilet;
08= Gents. Toilet; 09= Kitchen; 10= Snug Areas; 11= Vaults;12= Lounge; 13= Bar; 14= Fuel

Table 18.

Licensees of the Ferry/Unicorn in Gunthorpe

Period	Licensee	Period	Licensee
c.1695	Thomas Marshall	1919 to 1921	Leonard Gillborn
c.1716 to c.1725	Mary (Maria) Martin	1921 to 1923	Ivy May Wilson
c.1736	Joseph Taylor	1923 to 1935	Harry Wilson
c.1739	Thomas Martin	1935 to 1937 (04)	Kate Wilson
c.1753	Thomas Warne	1937 (04) to 1937 (07)	Ivy May Day
c.1760	Thomas Raynor	1937 (07) to 1938	Claude Hamilton Peake
c.1760	Robert Taylor	1938 to 1940	Camuon McAuslam Rice
c.1776 to c.1782	John Frith	1940 to c.1952	Thomas Walsh
c.1793 to c.1805	George Fountain	c.1952 to 1964	Harry Grange
1811 to 1815	James Riley	1964 to 1970	Wilford Bradley
1815 to c.1836	Thomas Marriott	1970 to 1971	William David Michael Eastlake
c.1836 to c.1855	Samuel Marritt	1971 to 1976	William Edward Gott
c.1855 to c.1871	Samuel Kirk	1976 to 1988	Trevor Scorer
c.1871 to 1880	Robert Thomas	1988 to 1990	Patricia Anne Knox
1880 to 1890	Thomas Hermon	1990 to 1991 (03)	Kevin David Brooks
1890 to 1892	George Andrew Ward	1991 (03) to 1991 (05)	Martin Wainwright
1892 to 1898	William Hefford	1991 (05) to 1991 (07)	Julian Roe Gammon
1898 to 1900	Hector Priestley	1991 (07) to 1993	Graham Hornigold
1900 to 1903	William Lambert	1993 to 1994	Bernadette Devine
1903 (02) to 1903 (05)	May Lambert	1994 to 1996	John Palmer
1903 (05) to 1904	Arthur J. Ward	1996 to 2001	Alison Carole G. Palmer
1904 to 1915	Henry Todd	2001 to 2004	Andrew James Coring &
1915 to 1918	William H. Edwards		Beverley June Dove
1918 to 1919	Charles deBerl Wells	2004 to	Catherine Heather Marian Bond

Between 1828 and 1861 there were seven coroners' inquests held at the Ferry/Unicorn [Miscellany Table 1.]. A précis of one is given below.

Man drowned in the River Trent: *On Tuesday the 20th May 1828 an inquest was held by Christopher Swann, Coroner, at the Unicorn, Gunthorpe, on the body of John Grocock. Edmund Godfrey, the Gunthorpe ferry-man, recognised the body to be that of John Grocock, boatman of Gunthorpe whom he had ferried over the Trent in his boat the preceding Monday evening, after 10'oclock. He said the deceased was rather in liquor he said "good night" and walked away towards East Bridgford without reeling or staggering. Samuel Turner of Newark was steering Mr. Hubbard's boat down the Trent on Sunday morning when he discovered the body near the Willow Holme. Mr. B. W. Wright, surgeon, of East Bridgford, had examined the body of the deceased and found a contusion over the left eye which he believed to have been occasioned by falling on a stone. This would have stunned the deceased so that he fell into the water, he would have been unable to help himself; there were no other marks of violence on the body. Verdict: Found drowned.*

Green Dragon

In 1782, an advertisement appeared in the Nottingham Journal, advertising the letting of a Malt Office in Gunthorpe, the negotiations to take place at the Green Dragon the house of John Parr.

To be Let *a Malt Office, in good repairs, in the County of Nottingham, conveniently situated by the River Side. Further particulars to the above Office may be known by applying to Mr. John Parr, at the Green Dragon, Gunthorpe[50].*

The Green Dragon existed until 1808 when the contents of the public house were sold, also included were two ferry boats for sale, one nearly new[51]. It must therefore be assumed that this public house must have been sited close to the river Trent. The landlord was James Riley; from 1811 he was the licensee at the Ferry/Unicorn.

8. Lambley

A number of alehouse keepers, operating legally or illegally, have been identified in Lambley during the seventeenth century. In October 1614/15, Henry Wyld was indicted for allowing his customers to take part in illegal games [playing cards] in his alehouse. His customers, John Cooper, William Ingleman, and Robert Spiby all residents of Lambley were also prosecuted. In January 1616/17, Robert Blacknall and Unwyn Turner, yeomen, were indicted for brawling in a tippling house. In July 1630, Brian Doughy and Dorothy Walker, victuallers, were indicted for breaking the assize of ale. In April 1632, Robert Brackennall, yeoman, was prosecuted for brewing without first obtaining a licence and four years later in April 1636, he was indicted for being absent from church and frequenting a tippling house. Emmott Doughty, a victualler in Lambley, was also prosecuted for entertaining Robert Brackenall.

During the next century, in the will of John Holmes [dated December 1718], he was described as a labourer and innholder. Later in this century, two public houses are named, the Butcher's Arms and the Parrot [see below].

To be Sold by Auction: *on Tuesday the 12th April 1774, at the house of Mr. Samuel Saxton the Butcher's Arms, at Lambley, in the County of Nottingham. A freehold close of full seven acres of good land, situate at Lambley aforesaid and now let at five guineas a year clear of all deductions whatsoever and as it is the old rent is capable of considerable improvement and the person who purchases may enter immediately on the premises.*
The auction will begin at three o'clock in the afternoon, when the conditions, which are few and reasonable, will be produced. The estate will be sold if there are two bidders to purchase the same[52].

Samuel Saxton was a butcher who came from Calverton to open a public house in Lambley, which he appropriately called "The Butcher's Arms". It is possible, that later it was re-named the Chequers when Saxton left Lambley. However in July 1774, he appeared before the Courts for allowing cockfighting to take place in his public house[53]. The charge, at the Quarter Sessions of the Peace, held at Shire Hall, on Monday the 3rd October 1774, *"that Samuel Saxton suffered several persons to be and remain gambling and cockfighting at his house"*. In January 1775, he again appeared before the Court, and asked for pardon and promising never to offend again. He was fined the sum of twelve shillings, and paying the fees and expenses of the prosecution, he was ordered to be discharged.

Pardon: *Whereas I Samuel Saxton of Lambley, victualler, at the last General Quarter Sessions of the Peace held at the Shire Hall in Nottingham, was duly convicted before William Coape Sherbrooke and Thomas Charlton two of her Majesty's Justices of the Peace. The charge was that I had suffered several persons to assemble at my dwelling house in Lambley for the purpose of gambling and cock-fighting. And the justices having set a moderate fine, enjoined me to make submission for my said offence in this public manner. I do therefore ask pardon of the public for the same and promise never to be guilty of the like again in the future. Witness by my hand this eighteenth day of January 1775[54].*

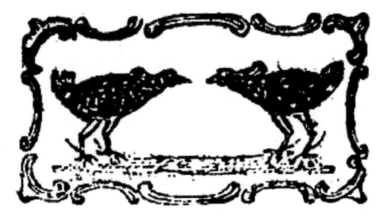

At this time, cock-fighting was perfectly legal, if it took place away from premises licensed to sell alcohol. It took many years, before this practice was made illegal; first in the Metropolitan Police District [1839], and the rest of the country in 1847. In 1952, an Act of Parliament was passed making it illegal to have possession of any instrument or appliance designed for the use in connection with fighting of any domestic fowl [cock-spurs etc.].

The other alehouse, which existed in Lambley, since at least 1761, was under the control of the Brownley family, Thomas, Joseph and Mordecai. It was called the Parrot and it seems very likely that it was re-named the Freemason's Arms early in the next century.

To be Sold: *To the best bidder on Monday the 19th day of October 1761, at the house of Thomas Browneley [Brownley] in Lambley, near Nottingham, betwist the hours of one and five in the afternoon, a close of four acres, more or less, of freehold estate. No less than half a guinea to be advanced each bidding*[55].

To be Sold: *By Auction at the house of Mr. Mordecai Brownley, the sign of the Parrot, Lambley, in the County of Nottingham, on Tuesday the 9th day of July 1799, between the hours of three and five o'clock in the afternoon. A close of old-inclosed land, in the Cottage Close containing six acres and two roods or thereabouts*[56].

The Lambley [formerly the Nag's Head, Chequers and possibly the Butcher's Arms]

8.1 Nag's Head 1997

First recorded in Alehouse Recognizances on the 10th September 1811, but may well have existed in the previous century, and as previously stated, it may have carried the name of the Butcher's Arms. The first mention of the Chequers, by name, was in the Nottingham Journal of 6th April 1816.

To be Sold by Auction: *At the house of Samuel Kirk, the sign of the Chequers, in Lambley, in the County of Nottingham, on Thursday the 18th April 1816 at three o'clock in the afternoon. About one acre and three roods of good land situate in Agram Well Coppice, tythe-free and exonerated from all rates and taxes*[57].

However by 1834 the Chequers had been renamed the Nag's Head a name which existed until very recently when in June 2004 it was styled "The Lambley".

To be Sold by Auction: *At the house of David Plumb, the sign of the Nag's Head, in Lambley, on Thursday the 6th day of March 1834 precisely at three o'clock in the afternoon. The sale is in three lots: Six convenient and substantial built dwelling houses, with suitable buildings and extensive gardens. A close of very excellent pasture land. Two closes of very excellent pasture land*[58].

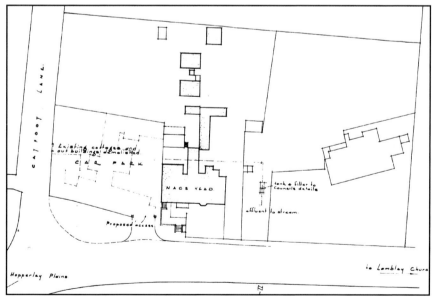

8.2 Site of the Nag's Head dated 29th July 1959

This public house remained in private ownership, well into the 20th century, but by 1959, it had been taken over by the Home Brewery. The new owners carried out a number of internal alterations, but the most fundamental was the demolition of the adjoining cottages and out-buildings to form the new car park. It is interesting to note, at this date, the club room had survived on the first floor. This room would have been the venue, over the years, for numerous meetings etc. For instance, a meeting of the Chartists was held there in August 1847[59]. Chartism was a movement, for political and social reform, in the United Kingdom in the mid 19th century. They followed earlier radical organisations, which demanded widening the franchise that came after passing of the Reform Act of 1832, which gave the vote to a section of the male middle classes, but not to the working classes. Public houses were often the venues for their smaller local meetings, having the facility of the much valued club room.

Table 19.

Licensees of the Lambley Public House [formerly the Nag's Head, Chequers and the Butcher's Arms] in Lambley

Period	Licensee	Period	Licensee
c.1773 to c.1775	William Saxton	1919 to 1931	James Robert Martin
c.1811 to c.1834	Samuel Kirk	1931 to 1955	Alice May Martin
c.1834 to c.1839	David Plumb	1955 to c.1959	William Thompson Martin
c.1839 to c.1843	Henry Barrowcliffe	c.1959 to 1966	John Hall
c.1843 to c.1847	William Richmond	1966 to 1978	William Peck
c.1847 to c1855	Thomas Shacklock	1978 to 1980	Jeffery Sale
c.1855 to 1861	John Watson	1980 to 1988	John Nicholas Souter
c.1861 to c.1864	William Stapleton	1988 to 1997	George Frederick Chamberlin
c.1864 to c.1868	John King	1997 to 1998	George Richard Chamberlin
c.1868 to 1872	Hiram Smith jun.	1998 to 2001	George Frederick Chamberlin &
1872 to 1884	John Scothern		George Richard Chamberlin
1884 to 1892	Alfred Hallam	2001 to 2002	Neil Austin Burgess
1892 to 1893	Hannah Hallam	2002 to 2003	Keith David Brand &
			Edana Romain Makin
1893 to 1894	William Bradley	2003 to 2004 (03)	Craig Brown &
			David Rodney Neaves
1894 to 1919	William Thompson	2004 (03) to 2004 (06)	Peter David Thompson
		2004 (06 to	Andrew Culkin &
			Mark Anderson

There were nine coroners' inquests held at the Chequers/Nag's head during the period 1828 to 1866 [Miscellany Table 1.]. A summary of one of these is given below.

Man died in a fight in a public house: *An inquest was taken on Wednesday the 28th March 1832 at the house of Mr. Samuel Kirk the Chequers, Lambley, before Christopher Swann, coroner, on view of the body of Joseph Godber, framework knitter, aged 66, It appeared from the evidence that on Saturday night about eleven o'clock the deceased and some others were sitting drinking at Plumb's the Robin Hood & Little John when a dispute arose between him and William Burrows, the consequence of Godber saying that Burrows did not take proper care of the church music books. The words "liar" and "fool" were used, when Godber struck the other who in return pushed him into the ash heap. The landlord and the other people in the house interfered to prevent any more violence, when Godber put out his hand as if to shake hands but instead of doing so took hold of Burrows by the collar and the neck cloth till he began to look black in the face. Burrows in self defence laid hold of Godber's collar and in the struggle Godber fell backwards and struck the back of his head against the table with such violence as to break off a large piece and then fell to the floor. Blood immediately gushed from his left ear and he was conveyed home in a cart, he never spoke but once, which was to his daughter, when she raised him up to give him some tea; he said " oh lay me down my wench I want to die". Mr. Wright Allen, surgeon, was sent for and he bled him but Joseph Godber died after noon on Sunday. On examination after death it was found that his skull was fractured over the left ear. It was evident that Burrows acted entirely in the defensive; neither party was much in liquor. Verdict: accidental death.*

Robin Hood [formerly the Robin Hood & Little John, the Freemason's Arms and possibly the Parrot]

This public house is recorded in 1811[37] in the alehouse recognisances of the 11th September, under the management of Elizabeth Brownlow [Brownley], but first mentioned by name as the Mason's Arms in 1818, when the licensee was Mordecai Brownley. However this inn was more widely known as the Freemason's Arms, but as previously mentioned above it seems very likely it had at one time been called the Parrot. From 1812 until 1831 records show that the licensee was Mordecai Brownley the younger. A further change of name to the property occurred in 1832 when the Freemason's Arm's was re-named the Robin Hood & Little John[60], a name which has survived until very recently when it officially became the Robin Hood, although this abridged version was sometimes used, as seen on the accompanying photograph. Locally it has always been known as the Robin.

To be sold by auction: *On Wednesday the 26th day of April 1815, at Mr. Brownloe's the sign of the Mason's Arms, at Lambley, in the County of Nottingham, at three o'clock in the afternoon. Seven acres of excellent pasture land situate near the lower end of Lambley leading to Oalbro' Wood, now in the tenure of Widow Burton.*

8.3 Robin Hood & Little John c.1900

In 1818, Mordecai Brownley the younger bought the Freemason's Arms from the then owner, George Newton, farmer and the trustees of a Mrs. Saunders. It appears that this inn had originally been two cottages[61]. The sale also included out-buildings, an orchard and garden; in addition, there was an adjoining dwelling house, currently occupied by Joseph Brownley [Mordecai's father]. The photograph [8.3] clearly shows the three cottages which now form part of the Robin Hood. Cottages attached to public houses were on occasions seen in villages [see the Plough and Old Ship Lowdham]. Mordecai was licensee of the Freemason's Arms until about 1832, when for a short period it came under the control of David Plumb who then went to the Chequers. It was about this time, that the Chequers public house was re-named the Nag's Head, and the Freemason's Arms changed its name to the Robin Hood & Little John. We may therefore surmise that Plumb was responsible for both these name alterations. By 1872 another farmer, William Screaton had bought the property; the Robin Hood & Little John had stabling, a bar, tap room, parlour and club room with an annual value of £18. In 1878 William Henry Hutchinson, Brewer, acquired a share in the ownership but by 1892 had gained full control and from 1916 the Home Brewery Company, were the owners, later Mansfield Brewery.

One event that caused a sensation in Lambley, was the arrest of Thomas Greensmith in the Robin Hood & Little John; he was suspected of murdering his four children in Basford. Apparently Greensmith came to Lambley, on Tuesday 4th April 1837, where he was known to the then licensee, John Brownloe [Brownley]. He spent the day in the public house, but in the evening he was recognised as the person wanted, in connection with this horrific crime, and he was arrested by the local constable and next day taken back to Basford, to face a Coroner's Inquest, where he was found guilty. At the subsequent trial the verdict was confirmed and Greensmith was sentenced to be transported for life to New South Wales[62].

Between 1832 and 1853 eight coroners' inquests were held at the Robin Hood & Little John [Miscellany Table 1.]. A précis of one is illustrated below.

Mother and son burnt to death: *An inquest was held on Tuesday the 23rd December 1834 before Christopher Swann, coroner, at Mr. Robert Godber's Robin Hood & Little John in Lambley, relative to the death of Samuel Culley aged five months. The child had burnt to his death when his cradle accidentally fell into the fire. His mother also received severe burns but she had been taken to Nottingham and died in the General Hospital. The jury returned a verdict of accidental death at the same time expressing the opinion that the father was highly censurable for leaving his wife alone for so long when he knew she was subject to fits and not capable of taking care of herself.*

Table 20.

Licensees of the Robin Hood [formerly the Robin Hood & Little John, Freemason's Arms and the Parrot] in Lambley

Period	Licensee	Period	Licensee
c.1761	Thomas Brownley	1894 to 1905	John Thompson
c.1794	Joseph Brownley	1905 to 1917	John Samuel Thompson
c.1799 to c.1811	Mordecai Brownley	1917 to 1920	George Linneker Clay
c.1811 to 1812	Elizabeth Brownley	1920 to 1923	John William Clay
1812 to c.1832	Mordecai Brownley the younger	1923 to 1925	Samuel Fell
c.1832 to c.1834	David Plumb	1925 to 1928	Thomas Laughton
c.1834 to c.1837	Robert Godber	1928 to 1930	Daniel Middleton
c.1837 to c.1841	John Brownley	1930 (02) to 1930 (12)	Richard Whanan Lamplough
c.1841 to c.1848	Thomas Brown	1930 (12) to 1932	Walter Morley
c.1848 to c.1855	William Savage	1932 to 1933	Stephen Custance
c.1855 to c.1861	William Green	1933 to 1944 (03)	Arthur Littleton
c.1861 to c.1869	David Plumb	1944 (03) to 1944 (04)	Annie Elizabeth Littleton
c.1869 to c.1871	William Screaton	1944 (04) to 1948	William Hall
c.1871 to 1873	George Reed	1948 to 1952	James Henry Woodward
1873 to 1879	John Harris	1952 to 1971	John Edward Fisher
1879 to 1881	Morton Handley	1971 (04) to 1971 (12)	Lavinia Fisher
1881 to 1884	Alfred Hallam	1971 (12) to 1988	Thomas Edward Woodcock
1884 to 1885	Samuel Parr	1988 to 1994	Beryl Cowpe
1885 to 1887	Eliza Parr	1994 to 1995	Derek William LaFear
1887 to 1889	James Kirk	1995 to 2007	Anthony George Beardsley &
1889 to 1894	Elizabeth Ball		Elizabeth Beardsley

The adjacent plan shows the Robin Hood & Little John in 1953. It will be seen that there were two rooms generally open to the public, a smoke room and a public bar. In addition the club room is still in place, which as in the majority of public houses under review would be used for general meeting etc. The skittle alley, another common feature of village hostelries, has still survived and it has only recently been demolished. There were other out-buildings, not shown on this part of the 1953 plan, but they were probably the old stables. During 2009, in the most recent refurbishment the interior of the Robin Hood [the new name] has been redesigned.

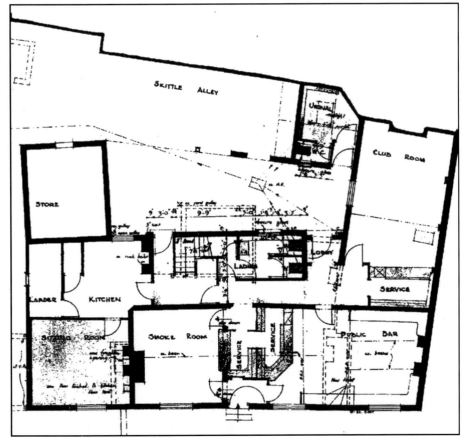

Plan 8 Ground Floor of the Robin Hood & Little John dated 17th November 1953

Traveller's Rest

This public house [on the edge of the parish of Lambley], first opened its doors about 1869. It was then licensed as a beerhouse, unable to sell spirits[63]. During the first year the then owner and innkeeper, Richard Smith, was prosecuted and fined 30s. for selling beer during prohibited hours. Initially the Traveller's Rest had stabling for four horses and six rooms, of which three were for public use; the annual value was £15. Richard Smith appeared to have been fined, on a number of subsequent occasions by the magistrates, for several misdemeanours, including allowing gambling, which was stated to be a serious offence. After Smith's death his widow, controlled the Traveller's Rest for a short period but then married William Bryan who then held the licence until 1900. The inn remained in private ownership until 1897, when it was acquired by Home Brewery, but it still remained a beerhouse, until a full licence was granted on 3rd March 1948[64]. A list of the licensees is given in Table 21.

Table 21.

Licensees of the Traveller's Rest in Lambley

Period	Licensee	Period	Licensee
c.1869 to 1876	Richard Smith	1930 to 1932	Herbert Powell
1876 to 1877	Elizabeth Smith	1932 to 1933	Harry Dewell
1877 to 1900	William Bryan	1933 to 1947	Mary Jane Donnellan
1900 to 1902	Elizabeth Bryan	1947 to 1952	Bertie Clarence Coates
1902 to 1905	Samuel Extall	1952 to 1953	Francis Maria Coates
1905 to 1917	Joseph Wood	1953 to 1967	Harold John Adams
1917 (05) to 1917 (10)	Mary Wood	1967 to 1982	George Eric Kent
1917 (10) to 1922	John William Thorne	1982 to 1987	Peggy Kent
1922 to 1924	Thomas Cartledge	1987 to 1988	Terry Saunders
1924 to 1926	Francis Sidney Parkin	1988 to 1997	Jeffrey Sale
1926 to 1928	Walter Chapman	1997 to 2001	Robert Jose Park
1928 to 1929	Joseph Henry Smith	2001 to 2002	Carol Collins
1929 to 1930	Frank Charlesworth	2002 to	Philip John Beale

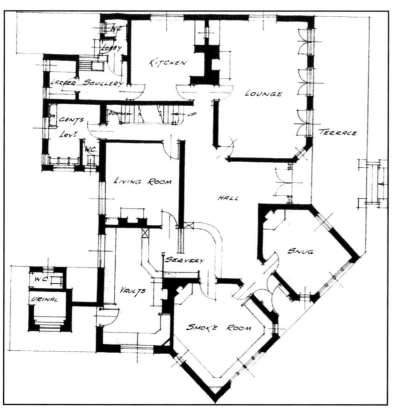

Originally The Traveller's Rest had three rooms open to the public. However as can be seen by the attached plan in 1948 there were four. This was a trend in many village public houses providing spaces for the various customers' requirements (separation of the classes perhaps). The trend today is just the reverse where one finds many pubic houses with a single large room. The Traveller's Rest appears not to have a club room. By 1948 the original stables had been converted into garages. The building was on three levels; on the lowest one were the beer cellar, bottle store and heating chamber.

Plan 9 Ground Floor of the Traveller's Rest dated 5th April 1948

White Lion

The first mention of this inn was in an advertisement in the Nottingham Review of 26th November 1852, although no innkeeper was mentioned, it seems very possible that this was David Plumb, who had, at one time, been the licensee of the Robin Hood & Little John, and then the Nag's Head in Lambley. He was listed as having a beerhouse on the 1851 census for Lambley and in the Trade Directory of 1855. Prior to being called the White Lion it seems very possible that it was known as the house of William Cooper from 1833 until 1848 [see the reference to a Beer-shop in Lambley below].

To be Sold by Auction: *At the White Lion Inn, Lambley, Nottinghamshire, on Tuesday 30th November 1852 at two o'clock, the following freehold property. Lot 1. Two messuages, workshops, yards and gardens, comprising more than 1000 yards of land, situate on the west side of Green Lane, Lambley, occupied by Samuel Plumb senior and Samuel Plumb junior. Lot 2. Two messuages, workshops, yards and gardens on the east side of Green Lane aforesaid, tenanted by Thomas Brown and William Adams*[65].

It will be noted that two of the advertised properties were situated, close to the White Lion, and occupied by Samuel Plumb senior and Samuel Plumb junior; possibly relations of David Plumb.

The next innkeeper of the White Lion was William Leafe, recorded on the 1861 census; he was also a framework knitter, and came to Lambley from Woodborough. It seems very likely however, that he was still in the latter village in 1857, as in that year his son, Thomas, was baptised in that place on 7th June. Therefore, it appears that he became a tenant of the White Lion, shortly after this event. A list of the licensees is given in Table 22.

Table 22.

Licensees of the White Lion in Lambley

Period	Licensee
c.1851 to c.1857	David Plumb?
c.1857 to 1901	William Leafe
1901 to 1902	John Henry Hogg
1902 to 1903	Joseph Perkins

This inn was originally a beer-shop under the terms of the 1830 Beer Act and only able to legally sell beer. However at the Brewster Sessions held at the Shire Hall, Nottingham on the 6th September 1865, William Leafe applied for a new licence, this was initially refused by the magistrates but on appeal the decision was reversed. Therefore, from 23rd of September in that year Leafe, beerhouse keeper and framework knitter, was granted a spirit licence[66]. He was resident at the White Lion for over 40 years. The property had stabling for four horses and featured a bar, tap room and club room. The annual value was £20. He appeared to have generally kept a well managed house, although he had one transgression, for in January 1871 he was fined for keeping a disorderly house. Although the White Lion had a club room, I have found little evidence in newspaper reports, apart from the one in 1852, [see above] of meetings being held there.

William Leafe left the White Lion on 2nd November 1901; he died the following year aged 87, and was buried in Lambley churchyard on the 30th July 1902, his wife, Charlotte, having died in September 1878. There were only two other licensees of the White Lion, John Henry Hogg and Joseph Perkins, but their tenure was short-lived, for on the 25th February 1903 the renewal of the licence was refused and the White Lion closed its doors[67].

The building was demolished some years ago and a bungalow erected on the site. A plan of Lambley in 1884 showing the position of the White Lion in Church Street is illustrated [Figure 8.4 page 41].

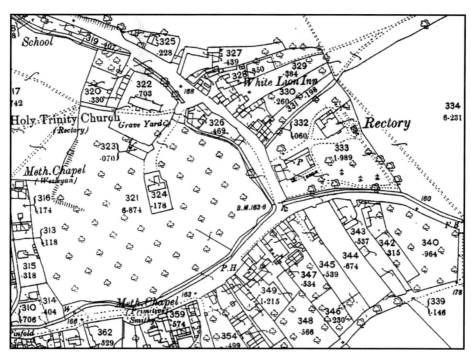

8.4 Lambley in 1884 showing position of White Lion Inn

Woodlark Inn [formerly the Dumble Tavern]

This inn appears to have been established about 1870, probably coinciding with the publication of the new licensing act of 1869, and the repeal of the Beer Act of 1830. The first licensee was Robert Plumb[68], but his residency

8.5 Woodlark Inn c.1900

was short-lived, for he died in 1875 aged 55 years, and on the 25th August of that year the licence was transferred to John Parr. The Dumble Tavern was a beerhouse and consisted of 16 rooms, four of which were opened to the public, with an annual value of £20. It also had stabling for four horses so it was a reasonably substantial property. However, Parr soon ran into problems for in 1876 he was prosecuted for tolerating drunkenness in his Inn and was fined 21s. by the magistrates. Eleven years later, in 1887, the name was changed to the Woodlark[69] and continues to bear this sign to this day. In 1892, the then Woodlark was purchased by William Henry Hutchinson, brewer [Home Brewery from 1916], but it remained a beerhouse until 1950 when on the 8th March of that year it was granted a full licence and for the first time in its history it was allowed to serve spirits[70]. Structural alterations to the premises were approved in 1997.

The list of licensees is given in Table 23. page 42 and a plan of the ground floor area of the Woodlark in 1950 is also illustrated [Plan 10. page 42]. This plan shows that the Woodlark had, at this time, two public rooms, in addition to the smoke room, there was a large vaults area divided into two by a central servery. The garden area is now the car park. A stream runs behind the public house, hence the earlier name of Dumble Tavern; the changed name of Woodlark appears to be rare in England. It is interesting to speculate why this changed name was chosen in 1887; it is unlikely to have a naval connotation, for the British river gunboat, HMS Woodlark, which saw service on the Yangtze River was not built until 1897. It seems most likely that the chosen name refers to the bird, Woodlark. Bird names for public houses have often been popular, and there are many examples, in fact there was an alehouse called the Parrot in Lambley in the eighteenth century [see page 34].

Table 23.

Licensees of the Woodlark Inn [formerly Dumble Tavern] in Lambley

Period	Licensee	Period	Licensee
c.1870 to 1875	Robert Plumb	1917 to 1921	Frederick Booth
1875 to 1877	John Parr	1921 to 1923	Samuel Fell
1877 to 1881	Alfred Hallam	1923 to 1924	George Parr
1881 to 1884	Samuel Parr	1924 to 1926	Charles Snowden
1884 to 1885	John Culley	1926 to 1949	Charles Price
1885 to 1887	William Humphrey	1949 to 1955	Ernest Cecil Winfield
1887 to 1891	Joseph Parker	1955 to 1958	Robert William Tom Custard
1891 to 1895	John Samuel Thompson	1958 to 1974	Harry Giles
1895 to 1896	Major Percival Griffiths	1974 to 1979	Terence Smart
1896 to 1905	George Radford	1979 to 1990	John Alan Verney
1905 to 1912	Joseph Radford	1990 to 1991	David Paulson
1912 to 1917	George Linniker Clay	1991 to	Michael Christopher Newton & Jill Newton

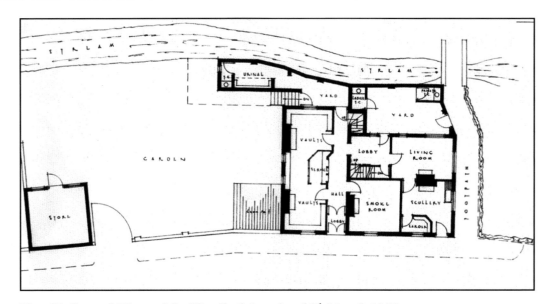

Plan 10 Ground Floor of the Woodlark Inn dated 8th March 1950

Unnamed Beer-shop

The house of William Cooper falls into this category it survived from c.1832 until Cooper's death in 1848 which was subject to a coroner's inquest [see below].

The premises of William Cooper were obviously fairly substantial as a sale of houses[71] and three coroners' inquests were held [1833 to 1848] here [Miscellany Table 1.]. One of these is illustrated below.

Sudden death from natural causes: *An inquest was held on Monday 30th October 1848, at the house of and over the body of William Cooper of Lambley. Ann Ancliffe, single woman, of Lambley being sworn said – I knew the deceased and have lived with him as his housekeeper for the last five years. He kept a retail beerhouse and was 76 years old. No other person lived in the house but us two. Between half past six and a quarter to seven o'clock on Saturday evening [28th October 1848] I went out to fetch a rabbit for our Sunday's dinner. I left the deceased sitting in the house-place reading a newspaper and no one with him. I was away about a quarter of an hour and on my return I found the house door just as I had left it. I went in but I could not see the deceased as the candle was out. I walked* *towards the settle and saw by the fire light that he was on the floor. I thought he had fallen in his sleep and I shook him calling out "master, master" but he never spoke. I tried to lift him up but could not. I turned his face towards the fire and saw his eyes were shut and his mouth open and that he was dead. I ran down the street and asked a young man to come but was afraid to touch the deceased and he was frightened at me saying "Mr. Cooper's dying". He did however help me to raise him up and held him until Mr. Hoffen, a neighbour came in. Mr. Thompson brought me some brandy and we tried to give the deceased some but he could not swallow. I took his cravat off and unbuttoned his shirt and rubbed his hands but he never showed any symptoms of life. It appeared to me that he had been taken suddenly ill and had fallen off his seat. The jury returned a verdict of sudden natural death and not otherwise.*

After the death of William Cooper, there is a possibility that his premises were acquired by David Plumb, which then became the White Lion.

9. LOWDHAM

There are a number of references to unnamed alehouses, in the seventeenth and early eighteenth centuries, in the Quarter Session proceedings held at Newark. In 1606, Robert Martyn was fined 5s. for brewing without a licence, and entered into a recognisance, the condition being that he should never in the future keep a victualling house. However, it appears that he was again brought before the Court, for drinking and playing games in an Inn during the period of divine service. In 1635, Thomas Saunderson, victualler, was indicted for keeping a disorderly house and fined 12d. Six years later, he was again prosecuted for allowing drunkenness in his house. Henry Alvey, labourer, was indicted for brewing without a licence in 1635 and fined 20s. and fined 5s. for being drunk. A warrant was issued to raise these fines; if he fails to pay he is to be whipped. James Brinsley was fined on a number of occasions, for brewing ale and keeping a common alehouse without a licence. A number of others were indicted for brewing without a licence, Richard Poate [Pawt], Margaret Beckwith, Mark Beckit, Henry Alley and in 1703 Sam Ffisher was fined £1 for selling ale without a licence. We have to wait until the end of the eighteenth century before definitive information about Lowdham public houses is found in the Quarter Session proceedings.

Bricklayer's Arms [otherwise known as the Brickmaker's Arms]

This was first recorded by name in 1866[68], as a beerhouse situated in the Main Street on the right of the Ship public house close-by one of Lowdham's brickyards. It may well have succeeded a beer-shop going by the colourful name of "the Sack-o-Taters" which was mentioned in a report of an affray associated with this brickyard in 1853.

9.1 Former Bricklayer's Arms 1997

Pump Riot at Lowdham: *On Wednesday the 20th April 1853, a formidable array of persons, of both sexes and of all ages and sizes, were charged before the County bench with assaulting and threatening Richard Harrison on Monday last. From the evidence of the witnesses, it seems that the complainant is the owner of a brickyard at Lowdham, by virtue of which he claims several yards of frontage on the road on which a pump was fixed. This having been erected some time ago, at the joint expense of the residents in the neighbourhood, they insisted upon enjoying the privilege of using it exclusively. At the latter end of last week, some unknown person, doubtless in the interests of the small tenants, removed the sucker to the chagrin of the irascible brick-maker, who could get no water, and to revenge himself did some further injury to the unfortunate pump, which had the effect of stopping the supply of the liquid element altogether. According to the testimony of a half-fuddled looking framework knitter, Thomas Stanley, an old man, who made himself the most prominent in the affray, declared at the "Sack-o-Tators" public house the same night that he would give Harrison a good hiding. Matters came to a serious crisis on Monday morning. As the complainant was walking away from his Yard, he was overtaken by Stanley, who took a large boulder and declared he would kill him. A quantity of persons, to the number of 30 or more, speedily collected together and stones and brickbats were fired in all directions, the target of course the unpopular brick-maker. A little ranter, named Joseph Browne, was especially* *abusive and threatening and very active with the stones. However the upshot of the proceedings was that the only serious charge was against William Stanley and the magistrates ordered him to keep the peace and to be discharged on paying costs of 52s. 6d. amongst them and promising not to molest the complainant again*[72].

Table 24.

Licensees of the Bricklayer's Arms in Lowdham

Period	Licensee
c.1866 to 1874	Samuel Paling
1874 to 1875	Eliza Paling
1875 to 1876	George Skinner

The Bricklayer's was a reasonably substantial building having eight rooms, four public rooms and stabling for five horses, the annual value was £10. Licensed to sell beer only, it ceased trading in 1876.

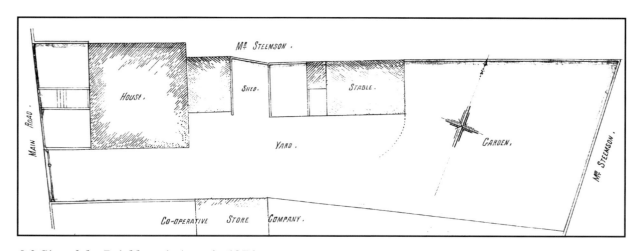

9.2 Site of the Bricklayer's Arms in 1874

At that time the then owner, John James Saxton, from Long Eaton a colliery agent did not renew the licence[68]. In 1874 Saxton had purchased the Bricklayer's from the owners Kirby & Ward, Brewers of Sheffield. Included in the conveyance document was a site plan, reproduced above. It shows that at this time the brickyard had been replaced by the newly erected Co-operative store, which had opened the previous year. As a private house it still stands in the centre of the village on the Main Street and the corner of Cranleigh Drive between the Old Ship public house and the Co-operative store. Some years ago a beer jug was found in Lowdham, which was impressed with the name Brickmaker's Arms. A photograph is reproduced on the left. It bears the name of the owner and so can be dated to 1874-76. [However, all the other documentation gives the name of these premises as the Bricklayer's Arms.]

9.3 Brickmaker's Arms Jug, impressed with the name of the owner John J. Saxton

Magna Charta

The first mention of this Inn by name, comes in 1835, when on the 20th February in that year, in an advertisement which appeared in the Nottingham Review, advertising a forthcoming sale of a cottage and land in Lowdham, at the

9.4 Magna Charta 1999

Magna Charta[73]. Later that year, a surviving deed records the sale of the Magna Charta, by John Foster and Henry Brett to Thomas Abbott of Marlock Farm, Lowdham, for £1,040[74]. The premises do not appear in the Alehouse Recognizances 1809 to 1826, or in the 1832 Trade Directory. It is very possible that the Inn was named after the Magna Charta Stage Coach, which began running from Nottingham to Scarborough on 26th August 1833, and which presumably passed through Lowdham, on its way to Southwell[75]. The first recorded innkeeper was William Dickinson in 1835, but his tenure was short-lived for he died on the 26th February 1839 from consumption [pulmonary tuberculosis]. His headstone survives in Lowdham churchyard. The list of licensees is given in Table 25 [page 46].

To be Sold by Auction: *At the house of Mr. Dickisson [Dickinson], the Magna Charta at Lowdham in the County of Nottingham, on Tuesday the 10th day of March 1835, at two o'clock in the afternoon. A cottage or tenement, with the barn, stable, outbuildings, yard, garden, orchard and appurtenances thereto belonging, situate at Lowdham containing three roods or thereabouts. Also three closes of pasture land with a hovel standing thereon situate at Lowdham containing by estimation seven acres and two roods. The premises are now in the occupation of Mr. George Knight Parr, who will show the same[73].*

**SACRED
To The Memory of
WILLIAM DICKINSON
Who died Febr 26th 1839
Aged 32 Years**

Fatal the fall. Assistance was in vain
Long was the struggle till death eased his pain
A sincere Friend and a Husband true
Stay and reflect for something more is due
Love, peace, harmony, adorned his mind
And left a character unstained behind

9.5 Transcript of the inscription on the gravestone of William Dickinson in Lowdham churchyard

9.6

The Magna Charta
Direct from Nottingham, by New Holland and Hull and Scarbro' in one day

The public are respectfully informed that this elegant four-inside Post Coach commenced running on Monday the 26th day of August 1833 leaving Mr. Hardy's at the Maypole Inn, Nottingham every morning (Sunday's excepted) at half-past five o'clock passing through Southwell to the Castle & Falcon, Newark and reaching Lincoln at half-past nine in time for the steam packet to Boston, thence through Spittal and Brigg arriving at the Cross Keys , Hull, the same afternoon at three o'clock in time for coaches to York , then proceeding to Beverley, Driffield and Burlington arriving at Scarbro' at ten o'clock in the evening.

Table 25.

Licensees of the Magna Charta in Lowdham

Period	Licensee	Period	Licensee
c.1835 to 1839	William Dickinson	1935 to 1940	Harry Joseph Pratt
1839 to c.1849	Mary Abbott	1940 to 1941	George Albert Smith
c.1849 to c.1868	Samuel Jamson	1941 to 1946	William Worthington
c.1868 to 1874	Francis Savage	1946 to 1952	Emiline Taylor
1874 to 1885	John Farley	1952 to 1958	Harry Hollis
1885 to 1888	Elizabeth Wooll	1958 to 1962	Thomas Lawton
1888 to 1892	Herbert William Pride	1962 to 1964	William Derbyshire
1892 (07) to 1892 (08)	Matilda Lawson	1964 to 1968	Lancelot Fredrick Green
1892 (08) to 1893	Joseph Orchard	1968 to 1975	Stephen Frederick Gunn
1893 to 1896	Matilda Lawson	1975 to 1981	John William Beamont
1896 to 1898	Edward Voce	1981 to 1991 (02)	Michael Wyler
1898 to 1899	William Pywell	1991 (02) to 1991 (11)	Patricia Ann Wyler
1899 to 1903	John Benjamin Willoughby	1991 (11) to 1993	Peter Stephen Skellett
1903 (02) to 1903 (11)	William Lambert	1993 to 1994 (03)	John Phillip Dandy
1903 (11) to 1905	Annie May Lambert	1994 (03) to 1994 (09)	Kelly Roberts
1905 to 1908	Joseph James Widdowson	1994 (09) to 1994 (12)	John Marsh Thompson
1908 to 1910	Miriam Featherstone	1994 (12) to 1997 (03)	John Eric McKeone
1910 to 1911	James Hitchcock	1997 (03) to 1997 (10)	Kevin Robert Varvell
1911 to 1914	Frank Atkinson	1997 (10) to 1998 (02)	Tony James Walker
1914 to 1926	William Kerry	1998 (02) to 1998 (05)	Virginia Rachel Kate Logan
1926 to 1934	Alexander Burgon	1998 (05) to 1998 (08)	Terrence Light
1934 to 1935	Albert Harold Samples	1998 (08 to 2011	David Desmond Davies

There were seven coroners' inquests recorded at the Magna Charta between 1842 and 1862 [Miscellany Table 1.]. One of these is summarized below.

A man killed at Lowdham in a fight: *A shocking case of death from violence took place on the morning of Wednesday the 24th April 1861. The name of the deceased was James Watson, a framework knitter aged 36 years. At the inquest held on view of the body at the Magna Charta public house on the following day, witnesses from the village were examined. Harriet Watson, widow of the deceased said when her husband finished work on the evening of 23rd he obtained his wages and went to the White Lion public house. At half past eleven o'clock, she went to this Inn, to fetch him home but he told her that he was not yet ready. She remained there until twelve o'clock, by this time he was in a very intoxicated state. There were with him, John Glazebrook, John Brown, Thomas Parkes, Joseph Bagguley, John Tuckwood, Elias Deabill and George Keeley. About one o'clock I went out again to fetch him home, but found him in the street quite speechless. John Glazebrook was putting his clothes on having stripped to fight her husband. Two men assisted her, to carry her husband to his house, and laid him on the floor, there was a bloody discharge coming from his nose. He did not recover consciousness and was dead by next morning. After his death she sent for Mr. Day, surgeon, and saw a large lump on the back of her husband's head.*

This was clearly a public house brawl, which spilled out into the Main Street in Lowdham, and there were a number of persons drinking and milling about at this late hour. From the evidence presented to the court over two days of the hearing, it seems that two contenders, John Glazebrook and John Tuckwood, were according to the jury, the culprits who struck the blows that resulted in Watson's death. They were committed, on a charge of manslaughter, to appear at the Nottingham Assizes. However, at their trial no further evidence was presented and the charge was dismissed.

As previously mentioned Samuel Abbott, a local farmer owned the Magna Charta from the autumn of 1835 but surviving records show that in 1872 the owner was John Marriott a surgeon residing in Colston Bassett. But in 1878 the then licensee, John Farley, bought the premises. Two other private owners are noted Elizabeth Wooll, also a licensee, and Nathan Pratt, a maltster, who sold the Magna Charta to Hansons Brewers of Kimberley. This Brewery owned the Magna Charta for 108 years until in 2006, Green King bought Hansons.

In addition to the sale of goods and land etc. and coroners' inquests the Magna Charta was the venue for holding statutes and for meetings.

Lowdham Statutes: *On Tuesday the 5th February 1850, a Statute was held for the hiring of servants, at Mr. Jamson's the Magna Charta Inn, Lowdham. We understand that the demand for agricultural servants was greater than could be supplied*[76].

In January 1851 the Annual Yeomanry Ball took place at the Magna Charta[77]. Some years later the landlord, Samuel Jamson, lost two fingers in a gun accident and as a consequence he developed tetanus. He was seriously ill for a long time but thankfully he recovered[78]. Over the years the lower reaches of Lowdham have suffered from floods due to the over-flowing of the Cocker Beck. Occasionally The Magna Charta was a victim. In 1857 there was a serious flood.

At Mr. Jamson's Magna Charta Inn: *The water rushed through the rooms, in a strong tide, filling the cellars and flooding other rooms in the basement. A fine pig weighing about 20 stones, the property of the landlord, narrowly escaped violent death by drowning. Mr. Jamson found the unfortunate animal in the stable, which was flooded to a considerable depth, keeping its head with difficulty above the surface of the water by the help of a wheelbarrow into which it had contrived to climb, and insinuate two of its feet, and by this means supporting the upper portion of his unwieldy bulk. It was speedily released from its perilous position and conveyed to a place of safety*[79].

One well-known personality came to Lowdham, after an illustrious career in professional football, playing for a number of clubs including Notts County 1947-52; his name, is Tommy Lawton. He was landlord of the Magna

Charta from December 1958 to December 1962. In his book *When the Cheering Stopped the Rise the Fall*, he says that although neither he nor his wife, Gay, had any previous experience of the licensed trade they took to it like ducks to water. He writes that the next four years, were particularly happy and to a great extent erased the unhappy memories and bitterness he felt about football. However, partially due to family commitments, and the fact that they were not receiving adequate recompense for the hard work of running a country pub Tommy and Gay, possibly reluctantly, left Lowdham for pastures new. The vacancy at the Magna was immediately filled by another Nottingham personality, William Derbyshire, but his tenure was not a long one lasting until October 1964. He had however previous experience of

9.7 Tommy Lawton

the licensed trade but his forte was in local government politics; he had been elected to Nottingham City Council in 1954. After he left the Magna Charta, his career flourished. He was elected Tory leader in 1964, then Lord Mayor and leader again from 1968 to 1972. He later became an Alderman. However, there is another man we should not forget, a very popular and very likeable landlord, Michael [Mick] Wyler was in charge of the Magna from December 1981 to February 1991. After his untimely death at an early age his wife Patricia Ann [Pat] looked after the pub for a few months until a replacement was found. Mick was sadly missed by many of his customers, and a large number flocked to his funeral in Lowdham, where he rests in the adjoining cemetery.

9.8 William Derbyshire

9.9 Michael Wyler

The Magna Charta has been altered and renovated over the years, [Plan 11. page 48]. This plan shows its ground floor layout in 1931; very much smaller than today. The original entrance to the yard is still in place where carriers' carts and stage coaches would have gained access. It is very likely that coaches passing through Lowdham would have called at this inn; it opened a year or so after the Magna coach, began its service from Nottingham to Scarborough in 1833. But the life of this coach service would probably not have lasted much more than about fifteen years. The opening of the Nottingham to Lincoln railway line in 1846 would, as in many areas of the country, lead to the demise of the Stage Coach. So it appears that the Magna Charta can be claimed as a former coaching inn, but for not very long. Outside the Magna Charta remained, until recently, one of the original mounting blocks, assisting gentlemen to mount their horses, or ladies to step down from a carriage or coach. Another feature of the 1931 plan is the tea room, a facility to attract families who would come out from the cities and suburban areas to the country, particularly during the summer months, travelling by train or charabanc or maybe by car. Undoubtedly, this room would have been used as the original club room, where meetings etc. would have been held in former times. A major renovation took place in 1992. The ground floor was enlarged, to form one room sub-divided into a bar area and a restaurant. An additional entrance was created into the car park and another into the newly created children's play area. The aim of the brewery was to cater for family diners and for traditional drinking. Additionally a large television screen was provided, for those customers wishing to view sporting programmes, principally football. A number of photographs of the interior of the Magna Charta, immediately prior to the alterations, were taken by the author and the one of the bar is reproduced below. In 2011 the interior of the Magna Charta was refurbished and the restaurant sub-divided into smaller units to create more intimate spaces for diners.

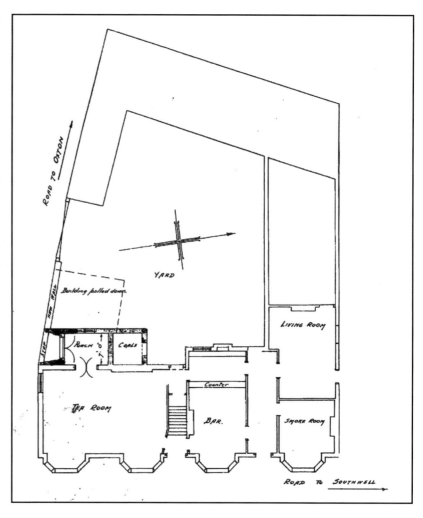

Plan 11 Ground Floor of the Magna Charta dated 11th April 1931

9.10 Public Bar of the Magna Charta 4th September 1993

Old Ship [formerly the Ship]

Surprisingly, the earliest records I have found come from the Churchwardens' Accounts for St. Mary's Church Lowdham, which record that they purchased ale from the local inns for the bell ringers[80]. Those which refer to the

9.11 Old Ship 1998

licensees of the Ship, cover the period 1788 to 1799. Unfortunately, earlier records have not survived. In the next century records are available from 1804. At the turn of the eighteenth century, the licensee and owner of the ship was Robert Porter the elder. He is also listed in the Alehouse Recognizances[37], from 1811 to 1820, after which the new inn keeper was Henry Woodward, and then Joseph Paling. When applying for a licence to be in charge of an alehouse, it was at this time, necessary to obtain a letter of support from the incumbent of the local church [see the transcript of one of these [4.4 p.24]. Robert Porter the elder remained as the owner of the Ship

until September 1835 when it passed to his son Robert Porter the younger although the latter never held the public house licence. On the death of Robert Porter the younger in December 1867, the Ship and the two adjacent cottages were sold for £600 and Thomas Steemson became the new owner[81]. The Ship, at this time was a substantial property, having a brewhouse, stable for 12 horses, outbuildings, yard, garden, and orchard. The inn had a bar, tap room, dining room and parlour with an annual value of £18. As with the other public houses in Lowdham auctions were held at the Ship.

9.12 Albert J. Pearce

To be sold by Auction: *At the house of Mr. Joseph Paling, Ship Inn, Lowdham, Nottinghamshire, on Monday, January 4th 1847, at four o'clock in the afternoon, subject to such conditions as will then be produced. All those two newly-erected cottages with gardens, together with that substantially built dwelling house, with orchard, barn, stables, hovels, piggery etc. For further particulars inquire of Mr. George Knight Parr, Lowdham, or Mr. J. Parr, builder, Southwell*[82].

The list of licensees is given in Table 26.

Table 26

Licensees of the Old Ship Inn [formerly the Ship Inn] in Lowdham

Period	Licensee	Period	Licensee
c.1788 to c.1799	William & Mrs. Foster?	1979 to 1980	Brian Smith
c.1799 to 1821	Robert Porter the elder	1980 to 1982	John Tongue
1821 to 1823	Henry Woodward	1982 to 1985	Ian James Potts
1823 to c.1861	Joseph Paling	1985 to 1990	James Harry Renwick
c.1861 to c.1871	Mary Paling	1990 to 1994	James Harry Renwick &
c.1871 to 1876	Thomas Steemson		David Francis Bowan
1876 to 1878	George Skinner	1994 to 1995	James Harry Renwick &
1878 to 1885	John Martin		Paul Gentry O'Donovan
1885 to 1899	James Seddon	1995 to 1996	James Harry Renwick &
1899 to 1904	William Wilkinson		Brian Rodney Saunders
1904 to 1910	Albert Joseph Pearce	1996 to 2005	Robert David &
1910 to c.1936	James Allen Kirkham		Nina Thompson
c.1936 to 1938	Mary Kirkham	2005 to 2006	Donald Clarke
1938 to 1940	Charles Walter Hardy	2006 to 2008 (03)	Dawn Clarke
1940 to 1949	George Booth	2008 (03) to 2008 (12)	Susan Joyce Green
1949 to 1975	Walter Anthony Higton	2008 (12) to	Margaret Mary Butler
1975 to 1979	Anthony John Harvey		

Albert Joseph Pearce [photograph 9.12 above] was the licensee of the Ship from 5th November 1904 to 3rd September 1910. He previously held the licence for the King's Head in Epperstone, from 2nd November 1901 to 5th November 1904. Pearce was a Nottingham man, born in Radford in 1865 and for a number of years worked in the lace industry prior to becoming a publican, a trade to which he returned after he left the Ship. He married Elizabeth Stevenson in 1901.

Two coroners' inquests were held at the Ship between 1829 and 1837 [Miscellany Table 1.]. One of these has been summarised below.

Accidental death of a child by scalding: *An inquest was held on Thursday the 26th January 1829, at the Ship, Lowdham on the body of Mary Graves, aged two years. On the 23rd December the child sat down on a pan of boiling water by which it was much scalded. For about a fortnight it was doing well, under the management of Mr. Billings, surgeon, who ordered dredging with flour; he however, discontinued his attendance when the mother refused to follow his advice, and used wax and oil. The child became worse and died on the 26th January. Verdict: Accidental death.*

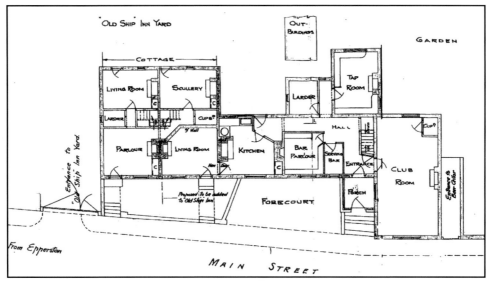

Plan 12 Ground Floor of the Ship dated 11th April 1925

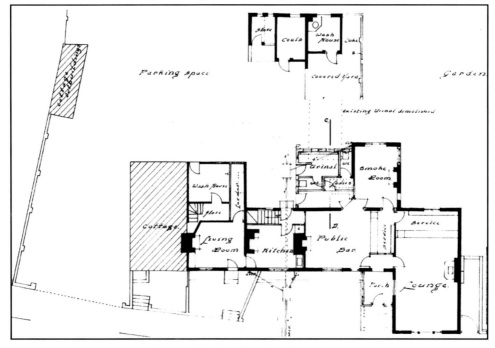

Plan 13 Ground Floor of the Old Ship dated 20th January 1953

To the left-hand side and attached to the Old Ship were two cottages. In 1925 [Plan 12. above] it was proposed that the one nearest to the Old Ship be added to the property and it seems that shortly after this plan was drawn this work was carried out. It is also interesting to note that at this date that the room to the right is still named the club room,

in 1953 this was re-renamed the Lounge, today it is the bar. Plan 13. dated 1953 on page 50 shows that the incorporation of the cottage has taken place but it was at this time still part of the living quarters, however some time later this area became a public space and today it is the restaurant. At this time, the second cottage was still standing, but was later demolished. The sketch of the interior of the Old Ship is interesting, as it shows that this room has little changed over the sixty years since it was drawn.

9.13 Sketch of the Interior of the Old Ship c.1950

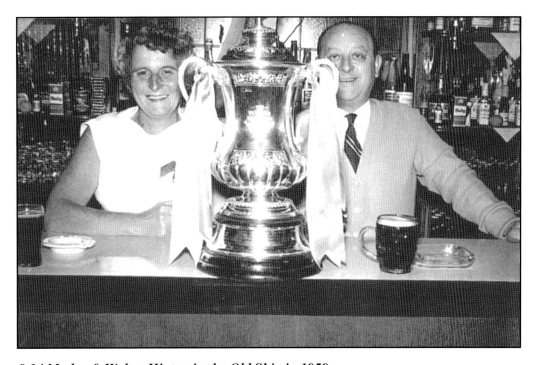

9.14 Madge & Walter Higton in the Old Ship in 1959

In 1959 Nottingham Forest Football Club defeated Luton Town in the Football Association Cup Final by two goals to one. The cup was brought into the Old Ship Inn for a brief display.

9.15 Old White Lion c.1920

Old White Lion [formerly the White Lion]

The earliest record (1783) to the publican, Andrew Savage, comes from the Churchwardens' Accounts for St. Mary's Church Lowdham[80]. As mentioned above, churchwardens routinely purchased ale, from local publicans, to be consumed by the bell ringers, on especial occasions. Later, in 1788, Savage appeared at the Quarter Sessions to give evidence for the parish of Lowdham in connection with a bastardy charge, against a third party for which he was paid £20[83]. In the Nottingham Journal of the 5th December 1807, an advertisement appeared for a sale by auction to be held at the house of Andrew Savage, the White Lion in Lowdham.

To be Sold by Auction: *At the house of Mr. Andrew Savage the White Lion in Lowdham, on Monday the 7th day of December 1807, at two o'clock in the afternoon. All those four freehold closes situate, in the Lordship of Lowdham, aforesaid, in a ring fence, in the occupation of Mr. Luke Teather, containing together by estimation 16 acres [more or less], called by the name of the Element Hills and lying opposite Epperstone Paper Mill on the west side of and adjoining the High Road leading from Lowdham to Epperstone[84].*

During the year after the above advertisement appeared, both Andrew Savage and his wife Elizabeth died; she on the 22nd May and he on the 28th November 1808. The licence of the White Lion then passed to Thomas Savage, who was in occupation until 1827. It has not been determined, who were the owners of the White Lion, during its formative years, but may have been held by the Savage family. By the beginning of surviving records, it is reported that ownership lay with Robert Abbott, described as a gentleman residing in Newark. In 1903, the White Lion was sold, and for the rest of its existence the new owner was John Trivett also from Newark. The White Lion, had stabling for three horses, a bar, tap room and club room, the annual value being £25. A list of licensees is given in Table 27.

Table 27.

Licensees of the Old White Lion [formerly the White Lion] in Lowdham

Period	Licensee	Period	Licensee
c.1783 to 1808	Andrew Savage	c.1871 to 1893	George Jackson
1808 to 1827	Thomas Savage	1893 to 1894	George Henry Groome
1827 to c.1832	Thomas Hill	1894 to 1896	Elizabeth Groome
c.1832 to c.1839	John Freeman	1896 to 1902	John Carlile
c.1839 to c.1851	Richard Weatherall	1902 to 1908	Elizabeth Lees
c.1851 to c.1861	Benjamin White	1908 to 1910	Enoch Smith
c.1861 to c.1869	William Grimley	1910 to 1917	Albert Radford
c.1869 to c.1871	Samuel Wilson	1917 to 1921	John Frederick Key

The White Lion [officially the Old White Lion from 1903] had sufficient room space to hold the occasional meeting and there were five coroners' inquests held here between 1832 and 1854 [Miscellany Table 1.]. A summary of one of these is given below.

A child choked on a marble: *On Sunday the 9th April 1832, at the house of Mr. John Freeman, the White Lion, Lowdham, on view of the body of Ann Wilson, aged eight months. It appeared in evidence that the deceased was the daughter of Wm. Freeman, cow doctor, Lowdham, and on Saturday morning, between eleven and twelve o'clock, the deceased was in the garden, under care of her sister, aged thirteen, who gave the infant a large marble to play with. The deceased put it into her mouth, and it got into her throat. The child was immediately carried to Mr. Billings, surgeon, but he was not at home. The apprentice, however, extracted the marble, but the child was dead. Verdict: Accidental death.*

When the renewal of the licence for the Old White Lion came before the magistrates in 1920, the police objected on the grounds of redundancy, in other words there were too many public houses serving the population of the parish of Lowdham. The report reads:

The Old White Lion is a fully licensed house situate in the Main Street of Lowdham, a parish with a population of about 950 inhabitants. The house contains two serving rooms, one being 13 feet by 10 feet and the other 14 feet four inches by 13 feet six inches and the average weekly sale of beer amounts to three 18 gallon casks. The rateable value of the house is £17. The premises are in a very dilapidated condition, but not in such a state as to render it unfit for habitation.

There are eight steps, leading to the entrance at the front of the house, and they are dangerous. There is a back door and also a side door to the premises. A contract for the sale of the premises was entered into last December [1919] but it has not yet been completed.

There are four fully licensed houses in the parish of Lowdham, in addition to the "Old White Lion", namely the "Ship" 100 yards away, the "Plough" 400 yards away, the "Magna Charta" 440 yards away and the "Railway" 755 yards away from the "Old White Lion". There is another public house called the "Volunteer" which is situated out of the parish but within a mile of the "Old White Lion".

The licensing authority refused to renew the licence on the grounds of non-necessity but agreed to issue a provisional renewal to run from 14th July 1920 to 26th March 1921 when the Old White Lion finally closed its doors[85]. So closed the only public house in Lowdham in private hands, all the others being under the control of the breweries. The house is now a private residence.

Railway Inn

9.16 Railway Inn 1998

This inn appears to have existed from at least 1847, as one of Lowdham's beer-shops, under the control of James Sears, who was also a coal merchant [a copy of one of his accounts is reproduced below]. The first reference to the name Railway, came in 1854, when Sears applied to the licensing authorities for a full alehouse licence, but he was refused and therefore he was only able to retail beer[86]. However, in 1872, under the new licensing system for alehouses, the Railway, now under the management of Samuel Martin, who ran the public house for 25 years, was permitted to sell spirits. This inn had stabling for four horses, a bar, tap room and a parlour; its annual value was £18. The Railway public house acquired its name through its close proximity to the Nottingham to Lincoln railway line, which was constructed through Lowdham in 1846. It was at this time owned by Thomas Barnard, a surgeon living in Epperstone, and then sold to Thomas Dufty of the same village passing to his widow in 1888. Early in 1903, James Shipstone & Sons, Brewers were lessees but on the 12th December 1923 the licensing authorities were informed that the Home Brewery Company now owned this public house. From 1999 Scottish & Newcastle, Pub Enterprises were the current owners.

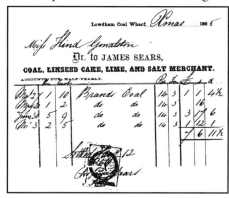

9.17 Account of James Sears 1868

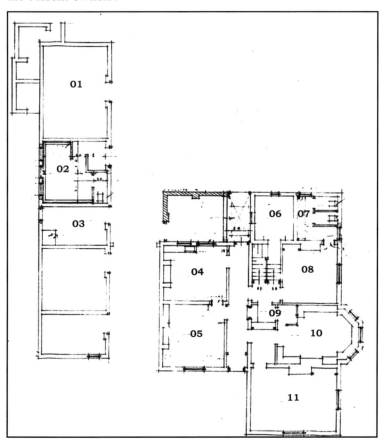

01= Old Stables
02= Gents. Toilets
03= Copper House [Wash Room]
04= Kitchen
05= Sitting Room
06= Store Room
07= Ladies Toilet
08= Lounge
09= Servery
10= Smoke Room
11= Tap Room

Plan 14 Ground Floor of the Railway Inn dated 6th May 1947

Although there were minor changes in 1951, and again in 1955, the layout of the ground floor of the Railway remained little changed from 1947 [Plan 14. page 53]. The out buildings, which originally would have been the stables, are still in place. In fact some have survived to this day [photograph below]. We have to wait until 1998-99 when a major renovation of the Railway took place and the individual rooms were amalgamated into one large room with a separate dining area at one end. This is an arrangement which is seen in many public houses today, for instance the Magna Charta and the World's End in Lowdham.

9.19 Out Buildings of the Railway 1999

9.18 Public Bar of the Railway 1999

9.20 Sketch of the Flying Scotsman

The photograph above left shows the cosy public bar of the Railway before it was swept away by the renovations in 1999. On the wall of the bar was a striking sketch of the Flying Scotsman this was the work of the then landlord, John B. Cook.

Also in the bar area were a number of railway memorabilia, which were very much in accordance with the name of this public house.

In earlier times one landlord, John Francis Hall, kept the Railway for twenty years from 1946 to 1966. The two photographs below show this smartly-dressed man behind the bar in the lounge and in his cellar.

9.21 John F. Hall in the Lounge Bar c.1960   *9.22 John F. Hall in the Cellar c.1960*

Table 28.

Licensees of the Railway Inn in Lowdham

Period	Licensee	Period	Licensee
c.1847 to c.1868	James Sears	1966 to 1977	Sidney Brooks
c.1868 to 1892	Samuel Martin	1977 to 1979	John N. Souter
1892 to 1898	George John Milward	1979 to 1991	Bernard Cater
1898 to 1901	Aaron Aldred	1991 to 1992	John Edward Storer
1901 to 1905	Harry Truman	1992 to 1998	John Broderick Cook
1905 to 1910	William Stanfield	1998 to 1999	David Ferguson &
1910 to 1912	Samuel Cowpe [Coupe]		Shirley Ann Murray
1912 to 1915	Joseph Arthur Brecknock	1999 to 2003	Amanda Margaret &
1915 to 1926	John Marriott Morley		Jeremy Francis Scorer
1926 to 1946	John William Henry Morley	2003 to 2004	Jane Heather Hill
1946 to 1966	John Francis Hall	2004 to	Michelle Ann &
			John Joseph Nimmo

Only one coroner's inquest was held in the Railway up to 1866, there may have been others at a later date, but this has not been investigated; the inquest in question was indeed a sensational one and relates to the suicide of the Station Master in Lowdham in 1861.

Suicide of the Station Master at Lowdham: *An inquest was held on the 9th May 1861, at the Railway public house, Lowdham, on the body of Leonard Moore. On Wednesday, he left home informing his wife that he was going for a walk, but when he did not return for his breakfast, she became alarmed. He was later found by the local police constable, hanging by his neck, in a hovel close to his house. Apparently contrary to his official instructions, he had given credit for some goods, and feared that he would not be reimbursed, before he had to declare his monthly accounts. This proved to be the cause of his distressed state of mind, and he left a note naming the persons, who owed him money. Verdict: That the deceased hanged himself during a period of temporary insanity.*

Springfield Inn

On the 23rd October 1945, planning permission was granted by Southwell Rural District Council, for a house to be built on Epperstone Road, Lowdham, with a proviso that the land was to be used for agricultural purposes. The building was completed by 11th December 1946, and the following year, the owner, Mr. Charles E. Dunthorne and his wife Winfred L., were in residence calling their new home "Springfield". They were market gardeners and sold produce including strawberries on the site. From a modest beginning the house was extended, but in 1974 they sold the property, and ten acres of land, to Mr. & Mrs.Gordon Ramsay Ferriman, which they occupied as a private residence until 1979. In this year they successfully applied for a magistrates' licence to sell alcoholic beverages and it opened as a licensed house on the 19th September 1979. Over the years improvement, expansion and conversion programmes continued. Mr. Ferriman and his wife soon established their restaurant trade, and it became renowned for fine cuisine in relaxing surroundings. The bars at the Springfield Inn were open to non-diners in licensing hours, and it therefore maintained a status as a public house. A feature of the Springfield in those first years was a large parrot in the entrance hall and outside there was a facility for landing a helicopter. It remained in private ownership until 1989 when it was sold to Courage [Brewery],

9.23 Springfield Inn 2001

later passing to Whitbread plc; it is now owned by Mitchells & Butlers. This is a modern public house, on the Old Epperstone Road, situated to the north-west edge of Lowdham parish. It is styled as a residential family public house and caters, primarily for those wishing to be served with meals, or take bar snacks and for those requiring overnight accommodation. A list of licensees is given in Table 29.

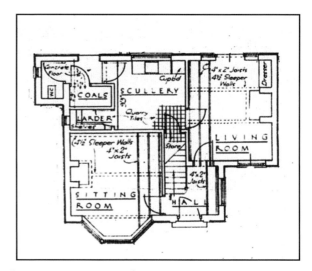

Plan 15 Front Elevation & Ground Floor of the Springfield House dated 23rd October 1945

The front elevation and the ground floor plan show the modest size of the Springfield when it was first erected and before it was greatly extended to become the large public house as it exists today.

Table 29.

Licensees of the Springfield Inn in Lowdham

Period	Licensee
1979 to 1989	Gordon Ramsay & Mavis Emily Ferriman
1989 to 1991	William Moore
1991 to 1994	Desmond Peach
1994 to 1996	Edward Roofe
1996 to 1998	Marcus Ramsdale
1998 to 2004-	Christopher Holdrick

World's End Inn [formerly the Plough Inn]

9.24 World's End Inn July 1989

The Plough was undoubtedly in existence in the eighteenth century. The earliest record I have found was in 1790 in the Churchwardens' Accounts for Mary's Church, Lowdham[80] when the then landlord provided ale for the bell ringers. Later, at the General Quarter Sessions of the Peace, held at the Kingston Arms in Newark on the 28th May 1794, the rules and orders and regulations of a Friendly Society, which met at the Plough, Lowdham, were confirmed and signed by the Clerk of the Peace[87]. At the time of the enclosure of the lands in Lowdham in 1766, a building is shown on the accompanying map, which equates with the position of the Plough Inn. This land was apportioned to Eliz. Sandys. It is therefore feasible to suggest, that the Plough dates from at least the middle of this century. The first recorded licensee was Robert Reason. He would have been aged 22 years at the time of the enclosure, so he, or another member of the Reason family, his father William perhaps, may well have been associated with Plough in these early years. He was baptised in Lowdham, the son of William and Rebecca Re(a)son, on the 30th June 1744 He married Elizabeth Chapman, on the 29th December 1783, also in Lowdham. Robert died on the 9th February 1804, and in his will he is described as a victualler, the beneficiaries being his two sons, Thomas and Robert and his three daughters, Mather, Hannah and Mary and his wife, Elizabeth. Robert's wife, Elizabeth, succeeded to the Plough subsequent to his death which she ran until 1812. The previous year her daughter, Hannah, married a blacksmith, Thomas Grocock, who came from Barkestone in Leicestershire and from 1812, he took over the licence of the Plough, and undoubtedly also carried on working as a blacksmith, a trade which in future years, continued to operate on the site, from time to time. Elizabeth Reason lived, with her family at the Plough, until her death on the 20th July 1848 at the great age of 95 years. In these early years sales and meetings and a few coroners' inquests were held in the club room [now swallowed-up by the families' living quarters] at the Plough Inn.

To be Sold by Auction: *On Thursday the 17th March 1808, at Mrs. Raison's [Reason's] the sign of the Plough, in Lowdham. All that freehold property, late in the occupation of Mr. Wm. Parkin, consisting of a house, bar, stable and other outhouses and about two acres of rich land, part of which is planted with choice fruit trees, situated in Lowdham, the land tax of which is redeemed and estate tythe-free. Sale to commence precisely at three o'clock in the afternoon*[88].

Thomas Grocock remained at the Plough for about 35 years for by 1848 he had been succeeded by another blacksmith, John Cragg, who came from Screveton, with his wife and young family. After his retirement from the licensed trade Grocock, continued to live in Lowdham with his wife, Hannah, until his death at the age of 79 years in January 1863, she dying three years later in May 1866, aged 77 years. By 1861 Francis Savage was the licensee and owner of the Plough, but in 1875 he sold this inn to Thomas Sears. Sears remained at the Plough until 1899 but he continued as owner until it was sold to Marston & Thomson, Brewers, Burton-on-Trent, so ending over a hundred years of private ownership. At the time of writing the Plough, now re-named the World's End, is owned by the Marston Pub Company.

In 1872 the Plough had three public rooms and two stall stables, the annual value was £17.

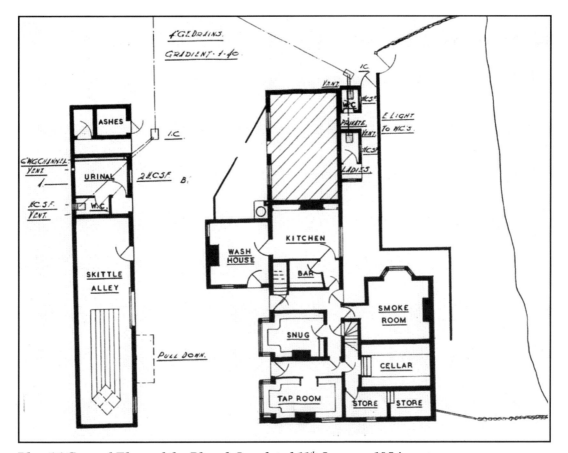

Plan 16 Ground Floor of the Plough Inn dated 11th January 1954

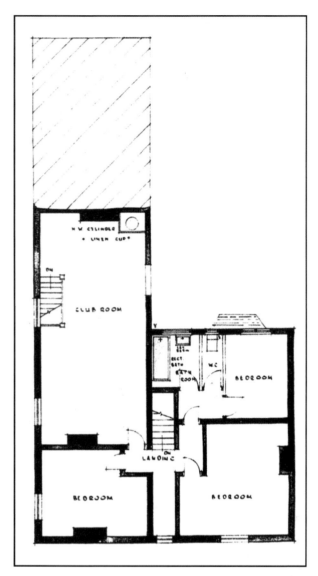

Plan 16. on page 57 is most remarkable in that it shows the Plough featured four public rooms. This was often a common arrangement, in earlier times, providing separate spaces, for disparate groups of customers. In larger pubs, in towns or cities, small windows were sometimes sited around the bars which could be closed to add privacy for customers; these were known as snob windows. Small rooms provided a similar facility. They were invariably given names as in this case, Bar, Snug, Tap Room and Smoke Room. A room jutted out into the car park, was marked as the Wash House but at a later date it was used as a kitchen. At the end of the Plough Inn was a small cottage shown as the hatched area. Outside there was a skittle alley, a very common facility in country pubs, This was originally the site of the blacksmith's shop but it was not demolished for some years, but re-used by Mr. Hibbert for shoeing horses. The first floor plan, of 1954 [Plan 17. on the left], shows that the large room known as the club room is still in situ. Major alterations to the Plough took place in 1966 when a bar and a lounge-bar were converted from four public rooms. The abutting kitchen and skittle alley/blacksmith's shop were demolished. The end cottage was also incorporated into the Plough and so gentlemen, for the first time in the pub's history, had the luxury of an in-door toilet. The next internal change took place in October 1991 when the bar and lounge were merged into a single room at the instigation of the then landlady, Christine Day. Some years earlier, in February 1973, the landlord, S. W. Grice, in connivance with the brewery, renamed the Plough as the World's End Inn. The car-park was extended and a huge flag-pole erected, not really in keeping with a rural pub [but now demolished]. A list of licensees is given in Table 30.

Plan 17 First Floor of the Plough Inn dated 11th January 1954

9.25 Plough Inn c.1950

9.26 Public Bar 19th October 1991

The left-hand photograph shows the Plough Inn before the renovations of the 1960's, the extension into the car-park is still in place. The right-hand photograph was taken just prior to the alterations which transformed the interior from two rooms into one. The then landlady, Mrs. Christine M. Day, is behind the bar.

Over the years, as one might anticipate, the Plough [now the World's End] has had very many regular customers and photographs of two of these are reproduced below.

9.27 Harry Reek in the bar of the Plough c. 1960's

9.28 J. R. Jeffery (Jeff.) in the World's End 9th April 2001

Harry Reek was a loyal customer for very many years; he lived in one of the cottages which bordered onto the Plough land; they were demolished in 1967 and new houses built on the site. Mr. Jeffery, always known as Jeff, was also a regular client of the Plough/World's End and the photograph was taken on or about his eightieth birthday.

Table 30.

Licensees of the World's End Inn [formerly the Plough Inn] in Lowdham

Period	Licensee	Period	Licensee
c.1790 to 1804	Robert Reason	1912 to 1927	Lydia Griffiths
1804 to 1812	Elizabeth Reason	1927 to 1928	Ferdinand Augustus Stones
1812 to c.1848	Thomas Grocock	1928 to 1944	George Anthony Higton
c.1848 to c.1861	John Cragg	1944 to 1948	Clarence John L. Wilkinson
c.1861 to c.1868	Francis Savage	1948 to 1954	Cecil Bird
c.1868 to c.1869	Mr. Norris	1954 to 1969	Hector Josiah Hibbert
c.1869 to c.1871	John Gunn	1969 to 1981	Stanley William Grice
c.1871 to 1874	William Wilson Butler	1981 to 1983	Terence Sidney Blood
1874 to 1875	Absolome George Barton	1983 to 1991	Alan Brown
1875 to 1899	Thomas Sears	1991 to 1994	Christine Mavis Day
1899 to 1901	Harry Leonard Stevenson	1994 to 1995	Paul Reginald Philips
1901 to 1908	John Morton	1995 to 2003	Stewart Donald Palmer
1908 to 1912	John Butler	2003 to	Susan Joyce Green

There were three coroners' inquests held at the Plough between 1834 and 1848 [Miscellany Table 1.]. A summary of one is given below.

A child was given sulphuric acid in mistake for laudanum: *An inquest was held on Monday 18th April 1836 at the Plough, Lowdham, on the body of John Allcock, aged four months. It appears that his mother routinely gave the child `Godfrey's Cordial' [laudanum] and finding that she did not have a supply she went to her uncle in order to borrow some. Unfortunately neither the uncle nor the aunt was at home and their daughter aged about 11 years gave her oil of vitriol [sulphuric acid] by mistake, which her father used for blacking. The mother of the diseased poured out half a teaspoonful and on placing it to the lips of the child he screamed out and pushed the spoon away. A surgeon was sent for but the little boy died at two o'clock next morning. Verdict: Accidental death.*

Named & Unnamed Beer-shops

9.29 World's End Cottages at the top of Red Lane

Under the terms of the 1830 Beer Act, a number of houses in Lowdham, applied for licences to sell beer, as with the other villages, the name of these premises and their location were only infrequently recorded, more often by hearsay only. In the 1832 Trade Directory, Joseph Burton was listed as having a beerhouse [beer-shop]. These persons were however, subject to similar legal restraints as the fully licensed alehouse keepers, and in that year Burton was prosecuted and fined 40s. for keeping his house open for the sale of beer at hours other than that allowed by law. In 1848 and 1853 James Sears was listed as a beerhouse [beer-shop] keeper and coal merchant & carrier, this seemed to be the fore-runner of the railway public house. John Sampson was listed on the 1851 census for Lowdham and in the 1853 Trade Directory as a beerhouse [beer-shop] keeper, his premises, the Sack-o-Tators, may have been a fore-runner to the Bricklayer's Arms. [see previous]. In 1852 a beer-shop keeper, called Charles Sampson, applied for a victualler's licence, but was refused at the annual licensing meeting. The name of his premises was given as the Star & Garter, in Lowdham. In 1853, William Widnall was listed as a beerhouse [beer-shop] keeper, but on the 1851 census his occupation was given as a huckster [a peddler or hawker]. These premises appear to have been at World's End [the right-hand house in the photograph] an out-lying part of Lowdham parish at the top of Red Lane. By hearsay it is said to have been called *The Traveller's Rest* but I can find up to the present no substantive evidence for this and it appears to have been short-lived, at least in the nineteenth century. William Tuckwood is recorded as owning a beerhouse [beer-shop] in the Trade Directory of 1864 and on the 1861 census for Lowdham is cited just the south of the railway line, by hearsay it was called the *Admiral Raglan*.

The Beer Act of 1830 was repealed in 1869 and these houses which were not within the magistrates licensing system either closed their doors or the occupiers applied for and were given or refused victuallers' licenses. Under the new system some were still only licensed to sell beer [beerhouse licence] or licensed to sell spirits in addition to beer [alehouse licence].

10. OXTON

From a search of the minutes of the Quarter Sessions, held at Newark-on-Trent in the 17th and 18th centuries, the names of a number of Innkeepers in Oxton have been noted. In 1609/10, Thomas Grubb, victualler, was indicted for allowing unlawful games to take place in his house. Later in the century, Thomas Grubb(e) was prosecuted, on three occasions between 1630 and 1634, for selling ale in quantities that were not in accordance with the law [breaking the assize of ale]. In 1630, Thomas Blatherwick was also prosecuted for a similar offence. Two persons were summoned to appear at the Quarter Sessions, for brewing ale without first obtaining a licence to do so, they were Mrs Richmond in 1613/14, and Thomas Clements in 1633. In 1634, Edward Singleton was indicted for allowing a fight to occur on his premises. During the next century, in 1703, William Taylor was prosecuted for selling ale without a licence. In 1727 five alehouse licences were granted in Oxton; they were to, Robert Marriott, Samuel Richardson, Thomas Cooper, William Smith and John Bush.

Blacksmith's Arms, Nag's Head and Plough

These three public houses appear in sale notices in the Nottingham newspapers in the 18th century but they do not again appear after 1800. We can only conclude that they closed as licensed premises or that the names were changed.

To be sold by Auction: *At the house of Richard Hallams, being the sign of the Blacksmith's Arms at Oxton in the County of Nottingham on Tuesday the 15th day of June 1773 at two o'clock in the afternoon, subject to such conditions as shall there be produced. One close called Hatfield Close, five acres and a half more or less. Grave's Hill Close, one acre and a half, by estimation more or less. Hunnenab Close, one acre and a half by estimation more or less. Fifteen acres of Arable Land, or thereabouts, lying in three separate fields, four acres are copyhold all the rest are freehold*[89].

To be sold by Auction: *On Friday the 1ˢᵗ day of July 1785 between the hours of three and five in the afternoon at the house of Mr. Weightman of Oxton, Nottinghamshire, known by the sign of the Nag's Head. The following copyhold estate within the parish of Calverton: The Broom-moor close 7 acres. The Grimes-moor Lane 2 acres. The Acre Head 3 roods. A common allotment 2 acres 1 rood & 14 perches. At the same time will be sold by auction together or in lots one hundred ash trees now felled on a farm called Holbecks in the parish of Southwell*[90].

To be sold by Private Contract: *On Friday the 7ᵗʰ May 1790 at eleven o'clock in the forenoon, at the house of Mr. William Ratcliff the sign of the Plough at Oxton, in the County of Nottingham, in two lots. Lot 1. One undivided fourth part or share of an inclosed freehold estate [tythe free] the whole consisting of an exceedingly good new farm-house with convenient out-offices and other necessaries and 115 acres of arable and pasture land well stocked with trees in a growing state and adjoining the house situate at Roffin Wood in the parish of Epperstone. Lot 2. One undivided fourth part or share of a certain wood called Open Wood adjoining the above farm containing 12 acres or thereabouts and consisting of about 1200 Oak and Ash trees chiefly Oak*[91].

Green Dragon

10.1 Green Dragon, Blind Lane, 1997

The first mention of this public house is seen in the Nottingham Journal of October 1787, although the inn keeper is not recorded it most likely would have been Joseph Steemson, who according to the Alehouse Recognizances 1811-12, was at the at the Green Dragon during this period. A few years earlier, in a newspaper advertisement of 1806, a Mr. Steemson was the licensee.

To be sold by private contract: *At the Green Dragon in Oxton, in the County of Nottingham, on Monday the 5ᵗʰ day of November 1787 six dwelling houses lying and being in Oxton aforesaid*[92].

Land at Oxton, to be sold by auction: *On Friday the 2ⁿᵈ January 1806, at the house of Mr. Steemson, the Green Dragon, in Oxton, at five o'clock, in the afternoon. In two lots:*
Lot 1. A close, or parcel of land, called Toothill Close, containing by estimation, 1 acre, 3 roods, 26 perches. Lot. 2. One other close, called Crisin Close, containing by estimation 1 acre, 2 perches[93].

Book of reminiscences of Oxton entitled: "I Lived in a Village": It features a publican who was licensee at the Green Dragon for many years. The Green Dragon Inn was the home of John Hopkin and his wife. He lived to be ninety-six years, and a year before he died he went up in an aeroplane. Old John and his brother James cooked the famous dinners for the Oxton Feasts at Whitsuntide[94]. He had a large family of boys and one girl. [He was the innkeeper of the Green Dragon c.1872 to 1890. He died c.1938.]

For many years, the Green Dragon formed part of the estate of the Reverend Henry Sherbrook, later passing to Captain William Sherbrook, both of Oxton. In 1891 the Home Brewery became lessees of the owners, finally gaining overall control in 1937. However, by the 1950's, the Nottingham Co-operative Society had purchased the Green Dragon, but by 1968 it had come under the control of Mansfield Brewery, and then Wolverhampton & Dudley Breweries in May 2003.

Originally the Green Dragon had nine rooms, four of which were open to the public. In addition, there was a facility to stable eight horses; the annual value was £16. The Green Dragon was obviously a fairly substantial building. The plans of 11ᵗʰ February 1955 [not illustrated for they are not suitably clear for reproduction], show that on the ground floor there was a lounge bar, a public bar and locals' room; on the first floor there was large café area. This latter room would, in former times, served as the club room. Over the years many meetings and functions were held in this room. Also this area would have also been used for holding coroners' inquests; during the period 1831 to 1860, ten were held at the Green Dragon [Miscellany Table 1.], an example is given below.

An inquest was held: *On Wednesday the 15ᵗʰ March 1831 at the house of Mr. John Miller, the Green Dragon, Oxton, on view of the body of George Hill. It appeared that the deceased resided at Halam and that John Wood his son-in-law, blacksmith, residing at Calverton, sent a cart with a lad about thirteen years of age, to fetch the deceased, to see* *his daughter. This was on Tuesday afternoon and the deceased sat in a chair in the cart. On descending Oxton Hill, the pony in the cart became restive and kicked; supposed to be caused by the breechband coming unhooked. The lad fell down and the pony ran away. When the cart was half-way down the hill one wheel of the cart went upon the bank and the deceased was thrown out and died almost immediately. His head was much cut. The pony stopped at the bottom of the hill. Verdict: Accidental death.*

The list of licensees is given in Table 31.

Table 31.

Licensees of the Green Dragon in Oxton

Period	Licensee	Period	Licensee
c.1787	Joseph Steemson ?	1941 to 1942	Leonard Dutton
c.1806 to 1813	Joseph Steemson	1942 to c.1956	Frederick William Smith
1813 to 1827	Richard Birch	c.1956 to c.1957	Raymond C. Porter
1827 to c1872	John Miller	c.1957 to 1963	John Aaron
c.1872 to 1890	John Hopkin	1963 to 1965	Ethyl Marjorie Wright
1890 to 1892	Harvey Hills	1965 to 1968	Geoffrey Wild
1892 to 1896	Charles Lynes Bates	1968 to1978	Donald John Rose
1896 to 1902	Adelaide Bates	1978 to 1982	Victor John Lewin
1902 to 1915	John Marriott Morley	1982 to 1997	Robert Reeves
1915 to 1916	Lawrence William Aitkin	1997 to 1999	Robert Dickson
1916 to 1918	John Hawksworth	1999 to 2000	Carol Broderick
1918 to 1921	Alfred Mays	2000 to 2001(02)	Mathew Robert Haywood &
1921 to 1924	John Willam Northage		Michelle Whetton
1924 to 1926	Arthur Hemmington	2001(02) to 2001(10)	Robert Reeves
1926 to 1941	Harry Bardill	2001 (10) to	Douglas Henderson Taylor

Royal Oak

The first mention of this Inn in Oxton was on Wednesday the 28th May 1794, in the minutes of the General Quarter Sessions of the Peace, held at the Kingston Arms in Newark. At this session the Rules, Orders and Regulations of a Friendly Society, which met at the Royal Oak in Oxton, were confirmed by the Justices and signed by the Clerk of the Peace[87]. In 1797 from an advertisement in the Nottingham Journal, it is noted that the Royal Oak was the venue, for the sale of houses in Oxton.

A dwelling house at Oxton to be sold by auction: *At the sign of the Royal Oak in Oxton aforesaid, on Thursday the 21st December 1797, punctually at two o'clock in the afternoon. The premises consist of a good cellar, house, parlour, kitchen and pantry with three chambers over the same, together with a yard, stable and other out conveniences thereto belonging. Also a small house or tenement adjoining the same. The above premises have been newly erected and may be entered upon immediately*[95].

10.2 Royal Oak, New Road Oxton c.1918

The building on the near right, in the above photograph, is the former Royal Oak public house, now a private residence. At the time of writing, the original cellar survives with the bench [stillage], on which the barrels of beer would be mounted and left to clear before being served [last used in 1871]. The other feature of this photograph is the sign *"Back way to the Young Oak Good Stabling"*. This refers to the public house, which was around the corner in Water Lane, the Young Oak, which closed shortly before this photograph was taken.

On the 30th November 1798 the Royal Oak was sold by then owners, William & Robert Hather & Samuel Grear, to John Brett[96], although the name of the licensee is not given and it is not until 1806, from an advertisement in the Nottingham Journal, that the name of Henry Moore is recorded. The subsequent licensees are listed in Table 32.

To be Sold by Auction: *At the house of Henry Moore, the Royal Oak in Oxton, on Tuesday the 11th day of February 1806, at two o'clock. A very substantial brick and tiled dwelling-house, a joiner's shop, timber yard and out premises, in the occupation of Edward Warren, also three good tenements adjoining in several occupations of James Pettiner, William Kirk and Samuel Samson. Also in one or more lots, three closes of excellent land near the Town End of Oxton, called Margaret's Close and also two closes adjoining called Foothill Closes. Possession of the land may be had immediately[97].*

Table 32.

Licensees of the Royal Oak in Oxton

Period	Licensee
c.1794 to c.1798	No record
c.1806 to c.1838	Henry Moore
c.1838 to c.1841	William Noble
c.1841 to c.1842	William Clarkson
c.1842 to c.1861	Emmanuel Duffield
c.1861 to c.1871	William Miller
c.1871	Thomas Allwood

The premises must have been reasonably large for during the period 1832 to 1858 eleven coroners' inquests were held there, [Miscellany Table 1.]. An example is summarised below.

Death through fear of rats: *An inquest was held on Thursday 9ᵗʰ December 1847 at the house of Mr. Emanuel Duffield, the Royal Oak Oxton, on the body of Sarah Lacey, whose death was caused under the following circumstances. William Bird of Oxton said that the deceased was about 70 years of age and lived alone in one of the parish houses. On Tuesday the 7ᵗʰ instant, about seven o'clock, he went to the deceased house having heard she was missing, and found the door locked and with assistance he opened it. On entering her bedroom, he found the deceased lying on the floor, almost naked and quite dead. She was deaf and he had often heard her complain of rats being in her room. About a fortnight ago, the deceased showed him her arms upon which were slight scratches, which she said were done by rats. Jane Burton said that on Tuesday morning week about half-past eight o'clock, she went to see the deceased as she heard her making noises during the night, by shaking a board and shouting that the rats had gone over her head, and were pulling at her feet. She looked in at the window, but saw nothing of her, so she supposed the deceased had gone to sleep again. She went away and heard nothing more until she was found dead. Verdict: Found dead from natural causes but accelerated by fear of rats biting her and falling down when she was alone.*

In its earlier years the Royal Oak was obviously a popular place for the holding of meetings. In 1808 a meeting of creditors met there and it was a routine venue for the Oxton Association, this being an organisation whose object was to reward its members who provided evidence for the successful prosecution of felons. Stallions were also brought to this Inn to be mated with the mares belonging to local persons.

The creditors of the late Richard & Mary Ratcliffe: *Late of Oxton in the County of Nottingham, are requested to meet the trustees, under the will of Mary Ratcliffe, at the Royal Oak, in Oxton, on Wednesday next the 21ˢᵗ December 1808 at 12 o'clock, in order to examine and investigate the property, and to determine the best means to be adopted for paying off the said Richard & Mary Ratcliffe's debts[98].*

Oxton Association for the prosecution of felons: *Will be held at the house of Mr. Henry Moore, the Royal Oak in Oxton on 1ˢᵗ January 1811 [A list of members is appended][99].*

Rewards

For house breaking £10.0.0
For highway robbery, horse, sheep or beast stealing £5.0.0
For killing or maiming of for any other felony or petty larceny £0.10.6

To Cover this Season 1810: *That high-bred horse Patriot, at five guineas blood mares, two guineas country mares, and 2s. 6d. the groom; the property of W. Wheatley of Watnall in the County of Nottingham.*
[A description of his breeding and his race achievements is appended].
He will be at the Royal Oak Oxton on Monday the 26ᵗʰ March 1810 at noon.
The money to be paid at midsummer next[100].

There are no further references to the Royal Oak, which was situated in New Road/Sandy Lane, after that recorded in the 1871 census return for Oxton, and one can only surmise that shortly afterwards this Inn ceased trading. The reason for its closure is not clear it is possible that the local magistrates refused to grant the Royal Oak a licence, under the terms of the new Act of Parliament which had recently come into force. However, the other two public Houses in Oxton, the Green Dragon and Bridge House, were both given their new licences at this date.

Ye Olde Bridge Inn [formerly the Bridge House]

Existed from at least 1841; on the census return in this year, Francis Burton is listed as a publican aged 40 years. It may however, have been opened some years earlier, possibly under the terms of the 1830 Beer Act. The name Bridge House first appeared in 1847 in the report of a coroner's inquest held there.

Oxon – Child Killed: *On Monday 4ᵗʰ July 1847 Christopher Swann held an inquest at Mr. Francis Burton's, the sign of the Bridge House, upon Thomas Paulson, four years old the illegitimate child of Maria Paulson of Radford. It appeared from the evidence of John Burton of Oxton, cottager, that on Saturday afternoon he was loading clover in his waggon and took his nephew, a child, and the deceased for a ride. He placed his nephew on the fore horse and the deceased on the shafts of the waggon and in this manner the children rode twice from the field. Burton went a* *third time to the field and again placed his nephew on the fore horse and the deceased on the shafts of the waggon telling him to hold fast, Burton walking by the side of the horses. When they had come about three quarters of a mile, he turned his head from the deceased to knock a fly off which was biting the horse, when the deceased fell off the shafts and the wheels passed over the child's head and killed him. The coroner addressed Burton on his thoughtless conduct, in placing a young child upon the shafts and expressed regret that in consequence of the law of deodands being repealed, he could not impose a fine. Burton, who appeared much distressed, said that he would never be guilty of such folly again. The jury returned the following verdict: Accidentally killed by being run over by a waggon.*

Auctions were also held at the Bridge House[101].

With the repeal of the Beer Act in 1869 the Bridge House came under the magistrates control as a licensed beerhouse;

10.3 Sketch of Ye Olde Bridge Inn c.1950

it was owned by the then tenant, Francis Burton who was presumably the previous owner. In January 1870 Francis died aged 75 years and his widow, Ann Burton, inherited the Bridge House and the tenancy. At this time there was stabling for six horses, eight rooms, three of which were open to the public with an annual value of £15. Ann Burton remained at the Bridge House until her death in December 1879, aged 82 years. By 1887 William Henry Hutchinson, Brewer of Basford [which became Home Brewery in 1916] had purchased the Bridge House. The plan below appears to show that this Inn had probably little altered since earlier times. The stables were still in place and there were also two adjacent pig sties. It was soon to be demolished and a re-vamped public house erected on the site.

In April 1929, Willie Shaw became the new tenant, and on the first of May in that year the name changed from the Bridge House to the Olde Bridge Inn[102]. However, it was still a beerhouse and not able to sell spirits and it was not until the 6th March 1937 that the licensing authorities saw fit to grant it a full licence[103]. On the 6th December 1999 Pub Enterprises, Edinburgh acquired the Olde Bridge Inn. A list of the licensees is given in Table 33.

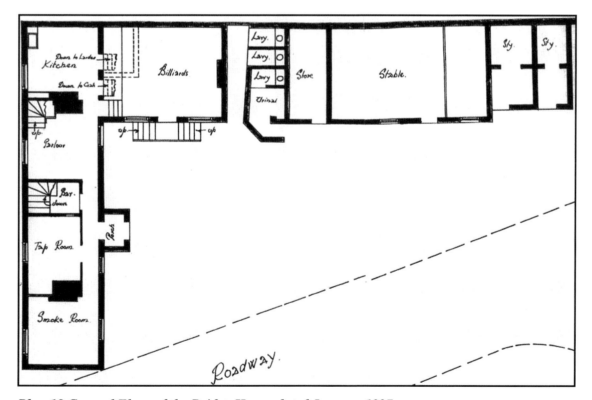

Plan 18 Ground Floor of the Bridge House dated January 1927

Table 33.

Licensees of Ye Olde Bridge Inn [formerly Bridge House] in Oxton

Period	Licensee	Period	Licensee
c.1841 to 1870	Francis Burton	1990 (02) to 1990 (05)	Ronald McKenna
1870 to 1879	Ann Burton	1990 (05) to 1990 (12)	Richard Jeffrey Jones
1879 to 1881	Edward Dyer	1990 (12) to 1991 (04)	Kevin Rose & Gary Lewis
1881 to 1887	James Moss	1991 (04 to 1991 (08)	Kevin Rose & Kevin Litchpick
1887 to 1899	George Colledge	1991 (08) to 1995	Kevin Rose & James Fleming
1899 to 1904	William Beardall	1995 to 1996 (06)	Kevin Rose
1904 to 1905	Elizabeth Beardall	1996 (06) to 1996(09)	Alan Hardwick
1905 to 1912	Edward Stales	1996 (09) to 1998	Maria Karen & Michael Colman
1912 to 1921	William Chettle	1998 to 1999	Kim Belsey
1921 to 1924	Edwin Jackson	1999 to 2000 (01)	Ian Cowling
1924 to 1927	Ethel Godley (née Jackson)	2000 (01) to 2000 (12)	Damian Robert Stanley
1927 to 1929	John William Northage	2000 (12) to 2001	John Barker
1929 to 1940	Willie Shaw	2001 to 2002	David Robert Greenhill
1940 to 1956	Charles Markham	2002 to 2003	Adrian Williams
1956 to 1966	Frank Ernest Barnes	2003 to 2005	Jeremy & Richard Lloyd
1966 to 1987	Percy Frank Bardsley	2005 to	Jane Ievins
1987 to 1990 (02)	Rupert Wilfred Richardson		

Two coroners' inquests were held at the Bridge House between 1847 and 1866 (Miscellany Table 1.), one has already been summarised above.

Young Oak

Emmanuel Duffield had been the licensee of the Royal Oak public house, in Oxton, for over 20 years, from about 1842. But by 1864, he had left these premises to open a new venture in Water Lane, Oxton[104], a beer-shop, initially under

the Beer Act of 1830, but in 1869 it had come under the magistrates control as a licensed beerhouse[105]. Unfortunately Emmanuel did not survive to profit from this enhanced status for he died in this year aged 70 years. Nevertheless, his widow Charlotte continued to run the business as both a beerhouse and a grocery, until shortly before her death, aged 76 years, in 1879. The Young Oak had been owned by the Duffields and it remained in private hands, until 1887 when it was bought by John Robinson, brewer of Daybrook[106], later transferred to the Home Brewery. The Young Oak had 10 rooms, four of them were open to the public, there was stabling for two horses and the annual value was £13. The Young Oak remained a beerhouse, an application, for a full alehouse licence in 1880 having been refused[107]. The photograph on page 63, taken c.1918, shows part of the other nearby former public house, the Royal Oak. It is interesting to note that the sign on the gable end of the building, which would have been the brew house, reads *"Back Way to the Young Oak Good Stabling"*. According to the photographer in 1918, A.J. Loughton, part of the Young Oak had been demolished and it was now a private residence. At the time of writing, this way through from New Road still survives and the brew house is now a private residence. As can be seen in the above photograph a building on the site of the Young Oak survives, probably somewhat altered from the original, but pleasingly named the "Young Oak".

10.4 The former Young Oak, Water Lane 2010

A list of licensees is given in Table 34.

Table 34.

Licensees of the Young Oak in Oxton

Period	Licensee	Period	Licensee
c.1864 to 1869	Emmanuel Duffield	1889 to 1895	John Souter
1869 to 1878	Charlotte Duffield	1895 to 1913	Edwin Patching
1878 to 1887	Joseph Gilbert	1913 to 1915	Alfred J. Davis
1887 to 1889	Henry Shaw	1915 to 1916	George Hubbard

At a meeting of the Licensing Authorities, on the 24th of February 1915, the future of the Young Oak beerhouse was discussed. They came to the conclusion that the licence was not required to meet the needs of the neighbourhood, in which such a licensed house was situated, there being too many public houses in the parish. They therefore, refused to renew the licence of the Young Oak. The current licence expired on the 23rd of January 1916 and compensation was paid to the owners[108].

11. WOODBOROUGH

In the minutes of the Quarter Sessions, held at Newark during the 17th century, there are a number of references to alehouses in Woodborrow [an earlier name for Woodborough]. The first was in 1607/08, when Henry Buck was indicted for allowing illegal games to be played although his occupation is not given, the event probably took place on licensed premises. During 1630 two victuallers, Edward Birket and Edward Trolove were fined for selling ale above the statutory price and in 1635 Thomas Crofts, was prosecuted for keeping a disorderly house, and likewise a labourer, Christopher Sellers, was indicted for drinking in an inn during the time of prayer. Unfortunately the signs of the alehouses in question are not recorded, but one further reference is of interest, relating to James Cliffe who was fined in 1660 for keeping a disorderly house. Was he the father of James Cliffe and the grandfather of Daniel Cliffe who kept the Bells public house during the next century, if so we can claim that the Four Bells was indeed a 17th century inn?

In 1727 three alehouse licences were granted, to Joseph Hodgers, John Charlton and James Cliffe. There are a number of other alehouse references in the Quarter Sessions and in the 18th century Nottingham newspapers. For instance in the Nottingham Weekly Courant of February 1762 the sale of a farm and land was advertised at the house of Daniel Cliffe at the sign of the Bells at Woodborough.

To be sold to the Best Bidder *at the house of Daniel Clift [Cliffe], known by the sign of the Bells in Woodborough: On Tuesday the 16th of February 1762, between the hours of one and three in the afternoon. A good farm house in Woodborough, with barns, stables and other convenient out-buildings, dovecote, malt kiln with convenient malt floors and rooms; a very good orchard and homestead containing upwards of two acres; one close of pasture in Woodborough of two acres and a small pringle [field] about a rood, together with 12 acres of arable land*[109].

There are further references to the Bells, in the newspapers between 1791 and 1799, by this time the licence had passed to John Gadsby. Between 1774 and 1798, Noah Wood features as the occupant of the Punch Bowl inn. In 1796 the Punch Bowl, was offered for sale; the schedule giving some early details about the size and layout of this public house.

In addition to the Bells and the Punch Bowl one other public house is recorded in the 18th century newspapers going by the name of the Boot and Shoe. This is the only reference to this inn that I have found, unless it was renamed the Punch Bowl under the patronage of Noah Wood from 1774 [see below].

To be sold by Auction: *On Friday the 24th May 1771, being the Friday in Whitsun-week, at the sign of the Boot and Shoe at Woodborough, six miles from Nottingham. A copyhold estate situate at Woodborough aforesaid, now in the tenure of Edward Gadsby, consisting of three tenements, barns and stable, an homestead of half an acre of good land and common rights for beasts, horses and sheep without stint. The auction will begin at four in the afternoon. This estate will be put up at sixty guineas, to bid two guineas each bidding, and it absolutely will be sold to the highest bidder*[110].

Bugle Horn

The Bugle Horn was established as a beer-shop in 1853, under the terms of the Beer Act of 1830[111]. After the

11.1 Bugle Horn c.1900

repeal of the above Act, it came, on the 10th August 1872, under the magistrates control as a licensed beerhouse, for the sale of beer only[112]. Joseph Leafe was the licensee, succeeded by his son Joseph Richard in 1886. Joseph was the brother of William Leafe who kept the White Lion in Lambley; their parents were Thomas [a framework knitter in Woodborough] and his wife Frances. Joseph Leafe owned the property, but probably for financial reasons, in 1878 Christopher Wyld of Woodborough had a part share, this passed to his widow, Susan Wyld in 1892 who by 1896 became the sole owner. In 1921 the licensing authorities debated the renewal of the licence for the Bugle Horn.

They reported:

The house stands on the Main Road in the village, nearly opposite to the church and contains three rooms which are used by the public, namely, a Bar 11 feet by 10 feet, a Parlour 27 feet by 10 feet 4 inches, at one end, and 14 feet at the other end, and a Tap Room 13 feet by 10 feet 6 inches. These are the only rooms on the ground floor and the licensee and his family use the Tap room as a living room. The house is in a dilapidated condition. The Parlour is in a very bad state, the brick floor having been worn away, the Tap room and bar have low ceilings. The walls of all the rooms have perished very badly. The brewhouse roof has fallen-in, in places, and the tiles have become dislodged. The brewing utensils are very old and have been there for many years. The urinal affords no privacy whatsoever. It is 10 feet away from the back door and 15 feet from the brewhouse wall.

In addition to the Bugle Horn there were, in 1921, three licensed premises in the parish of Woodborough, namely, the Four Bells a fully licensed house situated 66 yards away from the Bugle Horn on the west side, the Nag's Head, a fully licensed house 530 yards distant from the Bugle Horn on the east side and the New Inn a fully licensed house which is 900 yards away from the Bugle Horn on the north side. The Bugle Horn was the worst of the licensed houses from a structural point of view. Beer was brewed on the premises both at the Bugle Horn and the Nag's Head. All four houses sold about the same quantity of beer, that is to say, about 70 gallons each per week.

The police objected to the renewal of the licence in respect of the Bugle Horn on the grounds of structural deficiency and structural unsuitability of the premises and of redundancy. The view of the Licensing Authority was that premises of the Bugle Horn were structurally unsuitable as licensed premises. Having regard to these facts and also to the character and necessities of the neighbourhood, and to the number of licensed houses in the immediate vicinity, they were of the opinion that the licence which was now held in respect of the Bugle Horn unnecessary. Therefore, in the interests of the public, the renewal of the said licence was not desirable. The current licence expired on the 1st of April 1922 and the Bugle Horn closed its doors[113] and joined the Punch Bowl whose licence was refused to be renewed by the authorities in 1907.

The premises of the Bugle Horn were later demolished and a private house, built in 1978, now stands on the site.

Table 35.

Licensees of the Bugle Horn in Woodborough

Period	Licensee
1853 to 1896	Joseph Leafe
1896 to 1922	Joseph Richard Leafe

Cock & Falcon

William Hogg was a farmer, in Woodborough, and in 1823 he obtained a victualler's licence to open an alehouse at

his premises in the Main Street[114]. He continued to run his farm and the alehouse, which he styled the Cock & Falcon, until his death in May 1845, aged 58 years. The Cock & Falcon and farm were then managed, by his wife, Sarah, and his youngest son, William. Mother and son ran the Cock & Falcon until Mrs. Hogg died in April 1855 aged 69 years. However, tragedy had occurred in the family in 1847 when the wife of John Hogg, William's brother hanged herself at their farm in Woodborough and an inquest was held at the Cock & Falcon.

Suicide of a young married woman: *An inquest was held on Saturday the 25th September 1847, at Mrs [Elizabeth] Hogg's the Cock & Falcon in Woodborough, upon Elizabeth Hogg aged 28, wife of John Hogg, farmer of Woodborough. Sarah Richardson, aged 15, deposed, that she was a servant to the deceased. On the morning of the day prior to the inquest, Elizabeth Hogg brought her six-month old baby to her and asked her to wash and dress it, as she was feeling sick, and was going to lie down. When Mr. Hogg came in from his farm, for his dinner at twelve o'clock, he was told that his wife was upstairs. He went in search of her and found her in the garret; she was hanging by a noose, and was quite cold and dead. He fetched Mr. Osbourne, surgeon, and together they cut her down. It seems that for some time past she had suffered from pains in her head, which greatly troubled her. The jury returned a verdict of: Hung herself during a temporary state of insanity.*

11.2 Former Cock & Falcon 2000

Auctions[115, 116] and four inquests were held at the Cock & Falcon between 1831 and 1847 [Miscellany Table 1.]. It continued as a public house, until sometime in the 1860's, although William Hogg junior was still living at this address at the time of census return of 1871 but it appears that by now he was also no longer farming but listed as a collector of rents.

The Cock & Falcon remained a one-family concern and the reason for its closure is not clear. It is of course feasible it was refused a new licence under the terms of the new Licensing Act of 1869.

Table 36.

Licensees of the Cock & Falcon in Woodborough

Period	Licensee
1823 to 1845	William Hogg
1845 to 1855	Sarah Hogg
1855 to c.1865	William Hogg junior

Four Bells [formerly the Bells, Bell, Ring of Bells, Five Bells or Eight Bells]

The first definitive record to this public house in Woodborough was in 1762, when an advertisement appeared in the Nottingham Weekly Courant advertising that a farm house was to be auctioned in the Bells, the house of Daniel Cliff[109]. However 35 years earlier, it is recorded that James Cliffe obtained an alehouse licence. Genealogical searches, lead me to come to the conclusion, that James was the father of Daniel Cliffe, so possibly the Bells may have existed at this early date. It may have indeed been an alehouse at an even earlier date as it has already been recorded [see above] that James Cliffe was listed as a victualler in the Quarter Sessions of 1660.

11.3 Four Bells 1997

The sign "Four Bells" first featured in the 18th century, when it was recorded that a Friendly Society, met there in 1794[117], but for many years hence the other titles were sometimes used. The Four Bells was a reasonably substantial building, and appeared to be a popular venue for holding auctions of land and houses, and coroners' inquests. In 1872, it was recorded that it had seven rooms, four of which were open to the public. Also featured were stables to accommodate eight horses; the annual value was £18. For a number of years the Four Bells was owned by members of the church, they include Reverend Murray Wilkins of Southwell, Reverend Sherlock and Reverend Trebeck. By 1891 the Inn had passed into the ownership of the laity, and in this year it was sold. The new owner being Robert Halford an estate agent in Nottingham. In 1898 the Home Brewery bought the Four Bells and today the current owner is Pub Enterprises of Edinburgh.

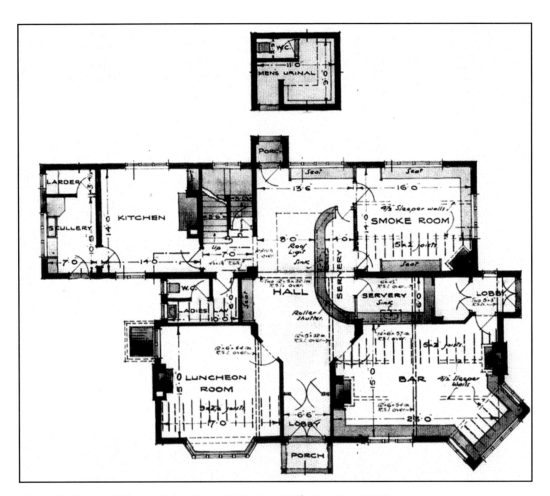

Plan 19 Ground Floor of the Four Bells dated 9th October 1926

To be sold by Auction: *On Monday, 23rd day of February, 1891 at 5 o'clock in the evening, at the "Four Bells" Inn, Woodborough, all that old established Inn called the "Four Bells", with Granary, Cart Shed, Cow-house, Stables and other out-buildings; also the orchard and croft occupied therewith; and containing in the whole three roods and twenty-four perches or thereabouts[118]. In addition there were another nine lots of land to be sold all in the occupation of Mrs. Emma Reavill* [the current licensee of the Four Bells].

Traditionally the occupants of the Four Bells had been farmers, and after the death of both, father-in-law William Reavill and her husband John, Emma Reavill acquired both the licence and the associated farm land. Shortly after the above sale Emma left the Four Bells.

Plan 19. on page 70 shows that in 1926, the Four Bells had three public rooms, one of which was a luncheon room designed to attract family groups who were visiting Woodborough. This was a facility which was also being incorporated into some other village public houses. It was in this year that the Four Bells was re-built.

11.4 Lounge Bar January 1999

11.5 Public Bar January 1999

The two photographs above were taken before a major interior conversion of the Four Bells during 1999, when the two separate rooms were merged into one; a transformation that was currently happening to a number of public houses in the area.

At one time publicans often remained as licensees for many years in the same hostelry. Clarence Levers served for 21 years, at the Four Bells between 1950 and 1971. The accompanying photograph shows him receiving a token of appreciation at his retirement in 1971. He was succeeded by Andrew Round and his wife Doris who between them ran the Four Bells for 28 years between 1971 and 1999. Doris Round retired in 1999.

A list of Licensees is given in Table 37.

11.6 Clarence Levers (second from the right) 1971

Table 37.

Licensees of the Four Bells in Woodborough

Period	Licensee	Period	Licensee
1660	James Cliffe?	1925 to 1926	Frederick Porter
1727	James Cliffe?	1926 to 1929	James Worthington
1762	Daniel Cliffe	1929 to 1931	Walter Hickin
c.1791 to 1832	John Gadsby	1931 to 1934	Ernest Anthony Chew
1832 to c.1855	William Gadsby	1934 to 1944	John Ernest Walker
c.1855 to 1884	William Reavill	1944 to c.1950	William George Robinson
1884 to 1887	John Reavill	c.1950 to 1971	Clarence Levers
1887 to 1891	Emma Reavill	1971 to 1978	Andrew Round
1891 to 1898	William Taylor	1978 to 1999	Doris Round
1898 to 1908	John Griffiths	1999 to 2001	Alan Thompson
1908 to 1912	Lydia Griffiths	2001 to 2002	Monam Elnager
1912 to 1916 (01)	Fred Woodward	2002 to 2004 (03)	Stephen Miles &
1916 (01) to 1916 (08)	Harold Boddy		Stephen Joseph Barratt
1916 (08) to 1922	William Taylor	2004 (03) to 2004 (11)	Stephen Miles
1922 to 1924	Thomas Jackson	2004 (11) to 2005	Stephen & Michelle Miles
1924 to 1925	John Herbert Williamson	2005 to	Stephen & Michelle Miles & Benjamin Shaw

Over the period 1831 to 1862 ten coroners' inquests were taken at the Four Bells [Miscellany Table 1.], a summary of one of these is illustrated below.

Child drowned in a pipkin: *On Wednesday the 29th August 1860, Mr. Coroner Swann held an inquest at the Four Bells Inn, Woodborough, on the body of Elizabeth Mellows, little girl about a year and a half old, the daughter of Samuel Mellows, a tailor. The child had met with her death the previous day under circumstances of a singular nature. A pipkin* [an earthenware jar] *about two feet deep had been set outside her parents' house to catch rain-water. The child being missed, a search was made for her, and at last the father found her lying in the pipkin and though the water in the vessel was only four inches deep, and she could not have been there no more than seven minutes, she was apparently drowned. Mr. Osbourne, surgeon, was sent for and in the meantime, the parents laid the body by the fire and rubbed it but on arrival of the surgeon he declared life to be extinct. There were some bricks by the side of the pipkin and it would appear the child had climbed onto them in order to ladle out some water with a little tin can she had in her hand and thus fallen in. The jury returned a verdict of accidental death.*

Half Moon

Paul Richardson was a grocer in Woodborough and at sometime during the 1830's he additionally began to serve his customers with beer on his premises which he styled the Half Moon. He undoubtedly obtained a Customs & Excise licence under the terms of the Beer Act of 1830. An advertisement in the Nottingham Review of 1839 shows that he was well-established, presumably as a publican in that year being supported by later entries in the Nottinghamshire Trade Directories. Although he continued to trade as a grocer he appears to have relinquished his victualling activities by the 1850's.

To be sold by auction: *Freehold House and Orchard at Woodborough at the sign of the Half Moon in Woodborough in the County of Nottingham, on Thursday the 26th September 1839, at three o'clock in the afternoon. All that newly-erected messuage or tenement, with the garden and orchard, well stocked with fruit trees, thereto adjoining and containing by measurement as now staked out, three roods and ten perches or thereabouts and in the occupation of the owner, Mr. Benjamin Greaves*[119].

Nag's Head

This public house appears to have been established about 1870[120]; it was owned by Noah Wood who farmed in Lambley and Woodborough. Whether, it existed at an earlier date is open to conjecture. In 1872 it was described

as having eight rooms four of which were open to the public and had stabling to accommodate four horses. The annual value was £19 19s. The Nag's Head was initially a beerhouse, but in 1874 it was granted a full alehouse licence, enabling spirits to be sold[121]. Noah Wood sold the premises in 1880 and the new owner was Roby Liddington Thorpe, a solicitor in Nottingham, passing to the Ecclesiastical Commissioners on the 10th May 1909. In 1924 it was bought by the then tenant, Arthur Shaw, but by 1956, it had been acquired by Hardy and Hansons, Brewers of Kimberley. The first licensee was Edward Robinson, but in 1875 the new innkeeper was 23 year old William Hogg, who remained as tenant for over 20 years.

11.7 Nag's Head 1997

At one time the Nag's Head had a lean-to extension on the right-hand side of the building, but in order to widen the road, this was demolished about 1927. Initially beer was brewed in the Inn, however by 1956, coinciding with the take-over by Hardy and Hansons, the brew-house was no longer functioning and in the plan below it is named as a store room.

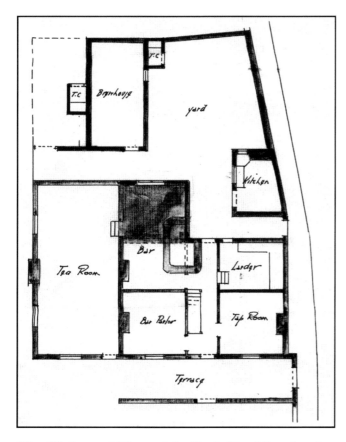

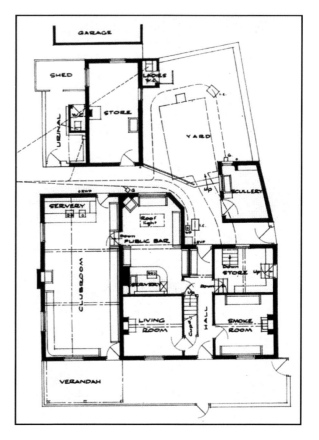

Plan 20 Ground Floor of the Nag's Head Inn dated 4th March 1927

Plan 21 Ground Floor of the Nag's Head Inn dated 5th July 1956

Table 38

Licensees of the Nag's Head in Woodborough

Period	Licensee	Period	Licensee
c.1870 to 1875	Edward Robinson	1963 to 1970	Hilda Redman
1875 to 1897	William Hogg	1970 to 1971	Alan Fowkes
1897 to 1898	Arthur William Whitehead	1971 to 1982	Stanley Caldwell
1898 to 1922	John Sears	1982 to 1990	Ray Fern
1922 to 1924	Arthur Shaw	1990 to 1993	Christopher Garth Binch
1924 to 1946 (06)	Arthur Frederick Shaw	1993 to 2000	Sally Jane Reacher
1946 (06) to 1946 (09)	Martha Shaw	2000 to 2003	Alan Ronald Cartledge &
1946 (09) to 1963	Thomas Redman		Marilyn Hill
		2003 to	Kenneth Kelly

New Inn

The New Inn, situated on Shelt Hill, was established by the time of the 1861 census return for Woodborough; the then licensee being William Harrison. Although it seems very likely that it was operative from about 1853, for Harrison's name is associated with a beerhouse listed in a trade directory of 1853[122], he appears on the 1851 census return for Woodborough as a cottager having 15 acres of land. In August 1861, the New Inn, with stables, cow hovels and other out-buildings together with seven acres and one rood of land was sold to a Richard Essam[123]. However it appears at some time later it was purchased by the then tenant, William Harrison, and after his death in August 1862, aged 52 years, the ownership passed to his widow, Sarah Harrison and remained in her possession until 1877. In 1872 the New Inn had eight rooms, four of which were open to the public. In addition there was stabling to accommodate four horses. The annual value was £15. The list of licensees is given in Table 39.

11.8 Former New Inn 2000

Table 39.

Licensees of the New Inn in Woodborough

Period	Licensee	Period	Licensee
c.1861 (or earlier) to 1862	William Harrison	1897 to 1899	Henry Hickling
1862 to c.1871	Sarah Harrison	1899 to 1902	Herbert Bunting
c.1871 to 1873	George Hardstaff	1902 to 1924	Willie Marshall
1873 to 1892	William Ashmore	1924 to 1926	George Henry Maltby
1892 to 1897	John Edwards Burton		

In 1926 the police objected to the renewal of the licence for the New Inn. At that time it was stated that the building was a very old one and contained three rooms which were available to the public, namely a Best Room, 11ft by 12 ft and 7ft 9ins high, a Tap Room, 12ft by 12ft and 8ft 3ins high and another room 8ft by 10 ft and 9 ft high. A portion of the passage was used as a serving bar only. There were 14½ acres of land to the house, 10 acres being grass land, 2½ acres a market garden and an orchard of two acres. The rent of the house was £28 and that of the land £42 a year, while the rateable value was £18 and £28-10-0 respectively. The licensee sold 18 gallons of beer, three bottles of spirits and half a gallon of port wine each week in winter and in summer the weekly sales were three 18 gallon barrels of beer, three bottles of spirits and half to one gallon of port wine. In addition the sales of bottled beer amounted to about 72 bottles per week. The costs of goods supplied to the New Inn between 1st May 1925 and 27th January 1926 were: Barrel Beer to Shipstones £305-16-7, to Offilers £45-15-0, to Nottingham Brewery £32-18-8 Spirits: to Chambers £48-3-3, to Skinner & Rook £40-0-0, to Kirkby £10-12-3½, to Marlow £3-10-0 Bottle Beer: to Skinner & Rook £49-9-5, to Home Brewery £55-18-8. Cigars, Tobacco etc. to Kirkby £13-8-2, to Waite £71-9-8, to Perkin £17-15-7.

George Henry Maltby, the current licensee, agreed that the profits from the public house were hardly enough to pay the rates and taxes of the house and he had to work at his market garden to make a living. There were two other licensed premises in the parish of Woodborough, the Nag's Head, a fully licensed free house 400 yards from the New Inn and the Four Bells a fully licensed tied house 1000 yards away. Both these houses are situated in the village and in a more advantageous position for catering than the New Inn. They also have better accommodation for the public and for vehicular traffic.

The view of the Renewal Authority was that, having regard to the character and necessities of the neighbourhood, and the number of licensed houses in the immediate vicinity, the licence for the New Inn was unnecessary, and that in the interests of the public the renewal of the licence is not desirable. The New Inn closed its doors soon after the refusal document was issued on the 20th April 1926 and compensation was refused[124]. The building survives as a private house today. Since 1877 the New Inn had changed hands on a number of occasions but at the time of closure the owner was Lady Charnwood Litchfield.

Punch Bowl

This is an 18th century public house from at least 1774 under the tenure of Noah Wood. In 1796 it was sold at an auction in Nottingham.

To be Sold by Auction at the house of Mrs. Lart, the Bell Inn, in the Market Place, Nottingham, on Saturday the 26th day of March 1796 at three o'clock in the afternoon. A freehold estate situated at Woodborough in the County of Nottingham and may be entered upon at Lady Day next. A good accustomed public house known by the sign of the Punch Bowl and now in the tenure of Noah Wood; consisting of four ground rooms, with chambers over them, a good arched cellar and a homestead containing three roods, 31 perches. There is also a most excellent garden, extremely well fenced and containing near half an acre. The said house if thought more convenient might for a few shillings expense be made into two dwellings, there being two pairs of stairs[125].

11.9 Former Punch Bowl, Main Street 1999

Noah Wood continued as the licensee of the Punch Bowl until his death in 1821; he was buried at Woodborough on the 2nd December of that year. His son Thomas then succeeded to the Punch Bowl until he died on Christmas Day 1841, the tenure of the Inn then passing to his son, Thomas, who maintained the licence until about 1860 when William Ashmore became the new tenant. In the early 1870's Ashmore took over the licence for the New Inn in Woodborough. However it appears that the Punch Bowl had been purchased at some stage by a member of the Wood family, possibly Noah, as early as 1796 when it appeared at auction [see above]. The family owned the Inn until 1883, their association of the Punch Bowl as tenants and or owners ending after a period of over a hundred years. Ownership remained in private hands for another ten years until it was purchased by Tom Gamble, Mineral Water Manufacturer in Nottingham and acquired by Home Brewery in 1898. The Punch Bowl returned into private hands after its closure as a public house in 1907. The property stands in the Main Street of Woodborough today.

In 1872 the punch Bowl had eight rooms; four of them open to the public. The stables could accommodate three horses; the annual value was £18.

At the Licensing Meeting held on the 28[126] February 1906 the renewal of the licence for the Punch Bowl was refused[126] and this public house finally closed on 2nd March 1907.

A list of licensees is given in Table 40.

Table 40.

Licensees of the Punch Bowl in Woodborough

Period	Licensee	Period	Licensee
c.1774 to 1821	Noah Wood	1892 (11) to 1894	John Allison
1821 to 1841	Thomas Wood the elder	1894 to 1895	Edmund Battersby
1841 to c.1860	Thomas Wood the younger	1895 to 1898	William Suffolk
c.1860 to 1872	William Ashmore	1898 to 1900	Jesse Charles
1872 to 1884	John Pollard	1900 to 1901	James Haynes
1884 to 1892 (04)	William Surplice Whitworth	1901 to 1904	William Housley
1892 (04) to 1892 (08)	William Reddish	1904 to 1907	James Taylor
1892 (08) to 1892 (11)	George Edward Harrison		

The Punch Bowl was sufficiently spacious to hold coroners' inquests for during the period 1847 and 1861 seven were held there [Miscellany Table 1.]. One of these is highlighted below.

Awful death of a Waterloo man: *An inquest was held on the 9th December and by adjournment on the 13th December 1861 at the Punch Bowl Inn Woodborough touching the death of John Atherley aged 65 years. The deceased was a pensioner, and formerly served in the Scots' Greys, with which regiment he fought at the battle of Waterloo. On the 2nd December he went to Nottingham, to draw his monthly pension, and on his return called at the Punch Bowl public house. Although he was then intoxicated he called for a pint of hot ale with three pennyworth of gin in it. After drinking that, he together with two or three boon companions, sat drinking gin and ale until the house was closed. The deceased was so drunk that he did not leave the house, but slept where he had had his last drink. The following morning he had tea and bacon for breakfast and during the day again got intoxicated. The following day [Friday] he appeared to be rather more sober, although the landlady, filled him two or three pints of ale. He went to bed in the afternoon and lay undisturbed until nine o'clock when the landlord, Mr. Ashmore, found him to be dead. There was no discoloration about the face and no discharge from the mouth. A small box containing opium was found in his pocket but Mr. Osbourne, surgeon, of Epperstone having made a post-mortem examination of the body, stated at the inquest that there was no symptoms of poison in the internal part of the body and that he had no doubt death had resulted from apoplexy [a stroke] brought on by excessive drinking. Verdict: Died from apoplexy brought on by excessive drinking and not by poison.*

Royal Oak

John Toplis opened a beer-shop, which he called the Royal Oak, in Woodborough soon after the publication of the Beer Act of 1830, which he ran with his wife Sarah. However, in 1845 the premises were sold and it seems that at this point Toplis ceased trading.

To be sold by auction: *On Monday the 17th day of February 1845, at five o'clock in the afternoon at the house of John Toplis, the sign of the Royal Oak in Woodborough, in the County of Nottingham, by the direction of the trustees of the Mr. Joseph Hucknall. A good substantially-built messuage situated in Woodborough aforesaid, with a garden, large yard, outbuildings and other conveniences which communicate with the public town-street; also a close of grass land adjoining, lately in the possession of Mrs. Mary Hucknall but now untenanted. Also the messuage, being the sign of the Royal Oak above referred to, now occupied by the said John Toplis as a retail brewery and which adjoins the yard belonging to the above premises[127].*

Unnamed Beer-shop

Charles Wood was a butcher in Woodborough who opened his house during the 1860's to sell beer, under an excise licence, in accordance with the terms of the 1830 Beer Act. At the licensing sessions, in September 1866, he applied to the magistrates to additionally sell spirits but was refused[128]. He possibly continued to trade until the Beer Act was withdrawn in 1869. In the 1871 census return for Woodborough, Charles Wood was listed as a butcher, and his premises described as a former beer house, next to the Wood Yard in the Main Street.

12. FINIS

Last Orders

12.1 Mary & Bill Grice, World's End Public House, Lowdham c.1975

Various Types of Public House Bars

Peterborough 1972

West Midland's Arms
Worcester 1973

Hearty Good Fellow
Southwell 1991

III. M I S C E L L A N Y

Table 1.

Coroners' inquests held in public houses between 1828 and 1866

Deceased	Age	Verdict	Reference
Unicorn in Bulcote			
John Kirkham	52	Found dead	N.R. 1831 (11/25) p.3.e
Foster (male)	<1 d	Died from haemorrhage and suffocation	N.R. 1849 (04/13) p.5.a.
John Clarke	child	Found dead in bed from natural causes	N.R. 1856 (12/05) p.4.e.
Henry Drury	32	Natural causes – epileptic fit	N.R. 1861 (04/05) p.8.a.
Cross Keys in Burton Joyce			
Elizabeth Dickinson	9 w.	Natural death hastened by want of proper food and attention	N.R. 1836 (01/22) p.3.f.
William Fairholme	40	Accidentally killed by falling from a waggon laden with corn	N.M. 1842(03/18) p.509.d.
Ann Mosley	3 m.	Smothered in bed she was overlain by her mother	N.M. 1843 (12/15) p.1237.b.
John Allcock	64	Found dead on the Midland Railway Line with certain injuries upon his body but there was no evidence to show how these had been received	N.R. 1847 (02/26) p.5.a.
Elizabeth Brownloe	68	Natural death by the sudden visitation of God	N.R. 1852 (01/30) p.4.c.
James Brewster	53	Natural death by the sudden visitation of God	N.R. 1857 (05/22) p.4.f.
Cornelius Scothern	child	Natural causes	N.J. 1861 (01/18) p.5.d.
Lord Nelson (formerly Swan & Salmon) in Burton Joyce			
Hannah Spyby	23	Hanged herself - felo de se - to be buried at night	N.R. 1833 (02/22) p.3.d.
William Ironmonger	35	Natural causes – visitation of God	N.R. 1833 (06/28) p.3.c.
Thomas Withers	39	Accidentally drowned in the river Trent	N.R. 1841 (03/05) p.6.d.
James Coalby	adult	Accidentally drowned in the river Trent	N.M. 1843 (06/19) p.329.d.
Joseph Jackson	4/ 9 m.	Accidentally drowned in the river Trent	N.R. 1847 (06/11) p.4.d.
John Clayton	13	Died from injuries he received, being kicked by a pony	N.R. 1851 (10/10) p.4.f.
Hannah Harby	66	Natural death by the sudden visitation of God	N.M. 1853 (01/14) p.5.a.
William Orchard	50	Found drowned in the river Trent but there was no evidence to show how he came to be there	N.R. 1857 (01/02) p.3.d.
Samuel Hubbard	4	Died from injuries he received from being accidentally burnt from the embers of a fire in a field	N.J. 1860 (06/08) p.5.c.
Thomas Kirkham	72	Natural causes	N.R. 1862 (05/16) p.8.b.
Wheat Sheaf in Burton Joyce			
George Mason	7	Accidental death by climbing on to and falling off the moving Newark coach	N.R. 1828 (08/01) p.3.c.
Sarah Brownloe	1	Naturally from a severe attack of cholera	N.R. 1854 (09/22) p.5.a.
William Sanders	2	Rupture of a blood vessel in the heart – Natural causes	N.J. 1855 (12/28) p.5.c.
William Hubbard	adult	Died on the road from natural causes	N.R. 1860 (11/16) p.5.f.
John Marshall	49	Natural death from natural causes	N.R. 1863 (01/09) p.5.f.
Emma Simpson	2	Natural causes – convulsions through dentition	N.J. 1864 (07/04) p.2.c.
Admiral Rodney in Calverton			
Mary Rounsevell	33	Cut her throat – insanity	N.R. 1828 (10/10) p.3.e.
No record (female)	<1d.	Still born – no evidence of the mother and how it came to be in the well	N.R. 1834 (11/21) p.3.e.
William Baines	8	Accidentally struck by a nog when playing skinny	N.R. 1835 (01/09) p.3.e.
John Fox	51	Natural causes	N.R. 1837 (12/22) p.3.d.
Jane Meads	8	Accidental death by burning	N.R. 1839 (09/13) p.4.e.
James Roe	7 m.	Died from suffocation in bed by rolling on his face	N.R. 1839 (12/06) p.6.b.
Charles Watson	23	Accidentally shot by a companion	N.R. 1840 (11/20) p.8.c.
Ann Watts	70	Natural death – apoplexy	N.R. 1843 (10/20) p.5.d.
Ann Meades	77	Natural death by the sudden visitation of God	N.R. 1845 (10/24) p.4.f.
Richard P. Franks	4 m.	Natural death	N.R. 1848 (05/12) p.4.d.
Elizabeth Rose	3 m.	Accidentally overlain in bed by his mother	N.R. 1849 (01/19) p.4.d.
Samuel Hind	5 m.	Natural causes accelerated by Godfrey's Cordial administered by his mother to procure rest	N.R. 1850 (11/08) p.5.a.
Nathan Meads	5	Found dead in bed from natural causes	N.R. 1851 (12/26) p.3.e.
James Smith	7 m.	Accidentally suffocated in bed	N.J. 1856 (04/18) p.5.a.

Table 1. (cont.)

Deceased	Age	Verdict	Reference
Admiral Rodney in Calverton (cont.)			
Elizabeth Allcock	78	Died from mortal injuries she received by being tupped by a ram. The ram has since been killed as it had attacked two or three other persons	N.R. 1856 (09/05) p.5.a.
William H. Burton	1/9 m.	Died as a result of accidental burns he received	N.J. 1860 (12/28) p.5.b.
John Gretton	74	Hanged himself during a period of temporary derangement	N.R. 1863 (01/30) p.5.f.
James Jackson	adult	Suicide by drowning and cutting his throat while in an unsound state of mind	N.R. 1864 (04/15) p.5.d.
Gleaners in Calverton			
Francis W. Cund	7 m.	Accidental death accelerated by a fall	N.R. 1858 03/05) p.4.f.
White Lion in Calverton			
Ann Cooper	3	Died as a result of accidental burns	N.R. 1835 (01/02) p.3.f.
Samuel Warrick	85	Natural death	N.R. 1835 (04/24) p.3.e.
Rose (male child)	14 w.	Natural death	N.R. 1836 (10/28) p.3.d.
William Lee	6	Died as a result of accidental burns he received	N.M. 1838 (02/17) p.53.d.
John Fox	4	Natural causes	N.R. 1839 (12/06) p.6.a.
Mary Farley	4	Died as a result of being accidentally burnt	N.R. 1842 (11/11) p.4.e.
Joseph Kirkham	33	Natural death from disease of the lungs accelerated by taking a large quantity of mercury	N.R. 1845 (05/23) .p.3.f.
Mary Fox	5	Died as a result of accidental burns she received	N.R. 1846 (01/01) p.4.f.
John A. Musgrove	7 m.	Died from the effects of an overdose of Godfrey's cordial	N.J. 1849 (12/28) p.5.e.
Wright (female child)	4 d.	Died from the effects of laudanum administered by her mother but with no evil intent	N.R. 1851 (06/20) p.4.e-f.
Benjamin Leafe	9	Sudden natural death	N.M. 1852 (02/27) p.4.e.
Mary Smith	8 m.	Found dead in bed from a convulsive fit and death was accelerated by the administration of laudanum for the purpose of producing rest but no evil intent	N.J. 1856 (03/20) p.5.c.
Robert Cooper	56	Sudden natural death and not otherwise	N.R. 1856 (06/20) p.6.d.
Elizabeth Roe	16 w.	Overdose of Godfrey's cordial with no evil intent	N.R. 1858(01/08) p.4.f.
Ann Hind	61	Found dead in bed from natural causes	N.R. 1859 (11/04) p.5.e.
Black Horse in Caythorpe			
Samuel Thompson	15 w.	Natural death accelerated by giving him a mixture of Godfrey's Cordial and Syrup of Rhubarb	N.R. 1851 (08/29) p.4.f.
William Stapleton	6	Accidentally burnt	N.R. 1854 (10/06) p.4.e.
Old Volunteer in Caythorpe			
Robt. Featherstone	21 m.	Accidentally drowned in a dyke	N.R. 1830 (07/02) p.4.c.
Elizabeth D. Morley	6	Accidentally burnt	N.R. 1839 (01/25) p.6.d.
Edward T. Wain	6	Accidentally drowned in a dyke at Lowdham	N.R. 1845 (03/07) p.3.f.
Jeremiah Charlton	7 m.	Died a natural death from want of food and the common necessities of life, not being provided by his mother, she being of weak intellect and being unfit to be trusted with the care of children	N.R. 1847 (03/19) p.4.e.
Harriet Stapleton	36	Natural death natural causes	N.R. 1849 (09/21) p.8.a.
William Wilson	70	Hanged himself was of unsound mind, he was a cow doctor	N.J. 1856(07/08) p.3.a.
Unnamed Beer-shop (possibly renamed the Black Horse) in Caythorpe			
George Savage	4	Found drowned in the Dover Beck but there was no evidence to show how he came to be in the water	N.R. 1845 (07/18) p.5.c.
Thomas Newton	65	Natural death by the sudden visitation of God	N.R. 1846 (12/04) p.8.d.
Mary Ann Tomlinson	25	Died as a consequence of cutting her throat she being of unsound mind	N.R. 1847 (01/22) p.4.f.
Cross Keys in Epperstone			
William Adkin	adult	Hanged himself in an unsound state of mind	N.R. 1829 (04/24) p.3.e.
John Mottram	37	Natural death	N.R. 1829 (07/03) p.3.d.
Mary Ann Jallands	3½	Accidentally drowned in a mill pond	N.R. 1834 (06/06) p.3.d.
George Wilson	5	Died as a result of accidental burns	N.R. 1836 (05/20) p.3.e.
John Blatherwick	77	Natural causes	N.R. 1842 (03/04) p.8.e.
Emma Plowman	3 m.	Died from the effects of laudanum and some other anodyne but with no intention to kill	N.R. 1842 (03/04) p.8.e.

Table 1. (cont.)

Deceased	Age	Verdict	Reference
		Cross Keys in Epperstone (cont.)	
John Joseph Burrows	3	Accidentally drowned in a tan vat – the jury recommended that these vats should	
		be fenced off to prevent this happening again	N.R. 1844 (11/15) p.3.f.
Sarah Johnson or Jamson	33	Died from excessive loss of blood naturally caused from breaking of a wound in	N.R. 1848 (12/29) p.4.f
		her leg	N.M. 1848 (12/29) p.5.c.
Joseph Smith	54	Found dead in a ditch from natural causes	N.R. 1849 (01/05) p.4.e.
George Barker	4	Died as a result of accidental burns	N.R. 1849 (10/19) p.5.a.
Ann Hemsley	81	Found dead in bed from natural causes	N.R. 1850 (08/09) p.4.e.
John H. Spowage	22 w.	Sudden natural death	N.R. 1854 (03/10) p.4.e.
		King's Head in Epperstone	
Mary Edith Harrison	3 m.	Natural causes – convulsions - congestion of the lungs	N.R. 1864 (02/26) p.5.d.
William Parr	77	Found dead in a field from natural causes	N.J. 1865 (03/02) p.2.d.
		Anchor in Gunthorpe	
Harriet Hunt	3 m.	Natural death natural causes	N.R. 1838 (04/20) p.5.a.
Mary M. Spurr	7 m.	Found dead from natural causes	N.J. 1840 (01/10) p.3.d.
William Grocock	82	Died from the effects of old age in a natural way	N.M. 1846 (10/23) p.5.b.
James Tomlinson	45	Cut his throat in a temporary fit of insanity	N.R. 1861 (04/05) p.8.a.
Kate Isabella Elliott	4	Accidentally died as a result of inhaling steam from boiling water in a kettle,	
		the inquest was held on Christmas Day	N.J. 1865 (12/29) p.2.f.
		Ferry/Unicorn in Gunthorpe	
John Grocock	adult	Accidentally drowned in the River Trent	N.R. 1828 (05/23) p.3.e.
John Walker	45	Natural death	N.R. 1834 (10/31) p.3.e.
John Ward	68	Natural death	N.R. 1835 (05/08) p.3.f.
Sarah Bailey	28	Natural death – spasms of the stomach	N.R. 1840 (02/28) p.6.d.
Sarah Ward	85	Natural death	N.R. 1855 (05/08) p.3.f.
Thomas Betney	21	Accidentally drowned in the River Trent	N.R. 1861 (08/02) p.5.c.
		Chequers/Nag's Head in Lambley	
Joseph Seston	7 m.	Accidentally drowned in the flood	N.R. 1828 (07/25) p.3.d.
Joseph Godber	66	Accidental death in a fight at the Robin Hood & Little John public house	N.R. 1832 (03/30) p.3.d.
Ann Plumb	44	Natural causes	N.R. 1837 (06/23) p.3.d.
John Selby	82	Natural causes – sudden visitation of God and not from poison, injury or violence	N.R. 1841 (01/01) p.4.e.
John Cooper	38	Natural death by the sudden visitation of God	N.M. 1842 (03/11) p.501.c.
Harriett Bridges	7	Sudden natural death	N.R. 1850 (03/15) p.4.f.
Mary Ann Walker	44	Sudden natural death	N.M. 1852 (03/05) p.5.a.
Martha Parnham	61	Natural causes	N.R. 1859 (11/25) p.5.c.
Jonathan Parr	71	Natural causes	N.R. 1866 (05/18) p.5.d.
		Robin Hood & Little John in Lambley	
Samuel Pepper	adult	Natural death by the sudden visitation of God	N.M. 1832 (02/04) p.1.d.
John Spencer	3 m.	Natural death	N.M. 1834 (04/05) p.108.c.
Samuel Culley	5 m.	Accidentally burnt to death	N.R. 1834 (12/26) p.3.d.
Thomas Cawthorne	30	Found drowned	N.R. 1839 (05/03) p.5.e.
Sarah Cooper	59	Died naturally by the sudden visitation of God	N.M. 1840 (08/21) p.272.c.
Hannah Raynor	63	Natural death natural causes	N.R. 1849 (02/16) p.4.c.
Hannah Nelson	18	Sudden natural death	N.R. 1850 (05/17) p.5.a.
William Burrows	79	Sudden natural death	N.R. 1853 (10/21) p.5.a.
		William Cooper's Beer-shop in Lambley	
Henry Hill	60	Accidentally drowned in a pond	N.R. 1833 (05/17) p.3.d.
Elijah Wright	2½	Died after being accidentally scalded from drinking boiling water from a kettle spout	N.R. 1835 (01/09) p.3.e.
William Cooper	76	Sudden natural death and not otherwise	N.R. 1848 (11/03) p.3.d.

Table 1. (cont.)

Deceased	Age	Verdict	Reference

Magna Charta in Lowdham

Deceased	Age	Verdict	Reference
Elizabeth Herring	4	Died as a result being accidentally scalded by drinking boiling water out of a kettle spout	N.R. 1842 (04/22) p.4.e.
Elizabeth Chapman	2	Found drowned in the Dover Beck but there was no evidence to show how she came to be in the water	N.R. 1845 (08/22) p.4.f.
John Chapman	adult	Accidentally killed on a railway line	N.R. 1857 (08/28) p.5.b.
Sarah Whatton	27	Natural causes (she died in Gonalston)	N.J. 1860 (06/08) p.5.c.
Thomas Huskinson	67	Found dead in a closet from natural causes by the sudden visitation of God	N.R. 1860 (12/28) p.5.e.
James Watson	36	Manslaughter against John Tuckwood aged 30, labourer and John Glazebrook, aged 23, framework knitter. However, at the Nottingham Summer Assizes both prisoners were discharged through lack of evidence	N.R. 1861 (04/26) p.8.b. N.R. 1861 (05/03) p.8.b. N.R. 1861 (07/19)) p.8.b.
Morris [or Blatherwick]	approx. 1 d.	The child was found suffocated in the soil of a privy but whether it was thrown in- there was insufficient evidence to prove	N.R. 1862 (10/03) p.8.a. N.J. 1862 (10/03) p.5.c.

Plough [re-named World's End] in Lowdham

Deceased	Age	Verdict	Reference
John Herring	adult	Sudden visitation of God – disease of the heart	N.M. 1834 (12/04) p.389.c.
John Allcock	4 m.	Accidental death as a result of being given oil of vitriol in mistake for Godfrey's Cordial	N.R. 1836 (04/22) p.3.e.
Hannah Dabell	2	Accidentally burnt - she unfortunately set fire to her clothes whilst warming herself in front of the fire	N.R. 1848 (02/25) p.4.e.

Ship in Lowdham

Deceased	Age	Verdict	Reference
Mary Graves	2	Accidental death by scalding	N.R. 1829 (02/06) p.3.d.
Mary Morris	5	Natural causes	N.R. 1837 (08/04) p.3.d.

White Lion in Lowdham

Deceased	Age	Verdict	Reference
Ann Wilson	8 m.	Accidental death as a result of choking on a marble	N.R. 1832 (04/13) p.3.e.
Ann Reddish	57	Natural death – to wit apoplexy	N.R. 1839 (02/15) p.6.e.
George Chapman	15 m.	Died in a sudden fit of passion but whether he choked on a piece of apple or not there was insufficient evidence	N.M. 1850 (09/06) p.4.e.
Elizabeth Greenfield	66	Natural causes – apoplexy	N.R. 1853 (02/04) p.4.f.
William Flinders	80	Sudden natural death	N.J. 1854 (06/02) p.5.d.

Railway in Lowdham

Deceased	Age	Verdict	Reference
Leonard Moore	31	Hanged himself during a temporary fit of insanity	N.R. 1861 (05/10) p.5.e. N.R. 1861 (05/17) p.8.e.

Bridge House (re-named Ye Olde Bridge) in Oxton

Deceased	Age	Verdict	Reference
Thomas Paulson	4	Accidentally killed by being run over by a waggon	N.R. 1847 (07) p.4.d.
Ann Wood or Ward	adult	Drowned herself in an unsound state of mind	N.R. 1862 (11/07) p.8.a. N.J. 1862 (11/07) p.5.a.

Green Dragon in Oxton

Deceased	Age	Verdict	Reference
George Hill	adult	Accidentally killed when his cart overturned	N.R. 1831 (03/18) p.3.d.
William Berridge	5	Accidentally burnt to death	N.R. 1833 (02/15) p.3.e.
Mary Walker	18	Natural death by the sudden visitation of God	N.R. 1838 (02/23) p.5.c.
Mathew Harvey	67	Natural death from natural causes	N.R. 1839 (02/22) p.6.d.
Elizabeth Greaves	38	Sudden natural death	N.M. 1846 (11/13) p.6.a.
Phillis Wain	73	Natural causes	N.R. 1847 (12/24) p.4.c.
George Martin	66	Sudden natural death	N.R. 1852 (07/23) p.4.f.
Hannah Gregory	58	Sudden natural death – disease of the heart	N.M. 1853 (12/23) p.5.a.
Emma Buxton	18 m.	Accidentally scalded from a can of boiling water	N.J. 1856 (05/09) p.5.b.
Francis Revill	54	Natural causes – visitation of God	N.R. 1860 (08/17) p.5.d.

Royal Oak in Oxton

Deceased	Age	Verdict	Reference
George Parr	22	Drowned himself in a fish pond, temporary derangement	N.R. 1832 (05/18) p.3.d.
George Berridge	23	Accidentally died after fighting – his skull was fractured	N.R. 1834 (08/01) p.3.e.
Thomas Bird	50	Accidentally fell from his cart and died from being run over by his own waggon	N.R. 1837 (07/21) p.3.f.
Luke Alsopp	79	Natural causes – sudden visitation of God	N.R. 1843 (02/24) p.8.d.
Sarah Lacey	70	Found dead of natural causes accelerated by fear of rats and falling down when she was alone	N.R. 1847 (12/17) p.4.d.

Table 1. (cont.)

Deceased	Age	Verdict	Reference
		Royal Oak in Oxton (cont.)	
Eliza Davies	31	Sudden natural death	N.R. 1850 (10/25) p.4.f.
William Barton	21 m.	Accidental death caused by narcotic substance presumably laudanum	N.R. 1853 (02) p.4.f.
Robinson (male child)	1 d.	Still born but illegally buried, the jury expressed their extreme disgust in the way the aunt of Miss Robinson had disposed of the body. On order of the coroner the body had been disinterred. The mother, Mary Robinson also died	N.R. 1854 (04/28) p.4.e
Esther Redgate	72	Natural causes by the sudden visitation of God	N.R. 1854 (06/30) p.4.f.
William Allcock	5 w.	Natural causes accelerated by laudanum given without any evil intent	N.R. 1856 (09/12) p.4.e.
Sarah Godfrey	10	Died as a result of accidental burns she received	N.R. 1858 (06/18) p.4.d.
		Cock & Falcon in Woodborough	
Mary Hallam	66	Natural causes – sudden visitation of God	N.R. 1831 (08/19) p.3.d.
George Green	40	Natural causes – sudden visitation of God	N.R. 1837 (01/27) p.3.d.
Ann Marshall	20	Natural death natural causes	N.M. 1843 (05/05) p.981.b.
Elizabeth Hogg	28	Hanged herself during a temporary state of insanity	N.R. 1847 (10/01) p.6.d-e.
		Four Bells in Woodborough	
Heziah Widdowson	4	Died of accidental burns he received	N.M. 1831 (11/12) p.365.c.
Edwin Wild	9	Natural death from natural causes accelerated by a fall against the church wall	N.M. 1842 (12/23) p.829.e.
George Leafe	11	Died from inflammation of the pericardium and pleura but whether such injuries were natural or caused by injuries inflicted on him by one John Smith the jury thought that there was insufficient evidence to prove	N.R. 1846 (11/27) p.8.e.
Hannah Smith	8	Natural death - cholera	N.R. 1849 (11/23) p.4.e.
David Orange	2 m.	Sudden natural death	N.R. 1853 (04/08) p.4.f.
William Alvey	2	Died as a result of accidental burns he received	N.J. 1855 (02/09) p.5.d.
Sarah Ann Cliffe	6 w.	Natural causes – died from convulsions	N.R. 1855 (06/08) p.4.e.
Baguley (female child)	<1 d.	Natural death from natural causes – not otherwise	N.R. 1856 (01/18) p.5.a.
Elizabeth Mellows	18 m.	Accidentally drowned in a pipkin placed outside to catch rain water	N.R. 1860 (08/31) p.5.d.
Harlock John	70	Died as a result of accidentally falling downstairs at home	N.J. 1862 (05/02) p.5.f.
		Punch Bowl in Woodborough	
William Jalland	24	Accidentally shot himself with a gun belonging to William Clay, farmer of Woodborough	N.R. 1847 (01/29) p.5.a.
Hannah Small	39	Sudden natural death	N.R. 1853 (12/09) p.4.d.
John Hind	3	Accidentally burnt	N.R. 1854 (02/03) p.4.d.
John Alvey	5½	Natural [his father was highly blameable for not hastening back with the medicine]	N.R. 1855 (12/07) p.4.e.
Ann Topliss	18	Died as a result of accidental burns she received	N.R. 1858 (08/06) p.4.e.
Mary Bradley	21	Died of haemorrhage through miscarriage but neglected by herself	N.R. 1860 (08/03) p.5.c.
John Atherley	65	Apoplexy brought on by excessive drinking	N.R. 1861 (12/20) p.8.a.

Abbreviations:

N.J. = Nottingham Journal
N.M. = Nottingham Mercury
N.R. = Nottingham Review

References:
The figures in brackets denote the month/day, succeeded by the page number and column number.

Source of photographs, figures and maps

Reference	Source	Reference	Source
0.1	NA (C/QDLV/4/7/10/2)	9.10	Author
0.2	LSL The Owl No.4 (1900)	9.11	Author
0.3	The Friendly Visitor, Vol. XXX11 (1899), p.173.	9.12	Mr. A. Pearce
1.1	LSL (19856)	9.13	LSL (Roulstone)
2.1	Author	9.14	Mr. J. R. Jeffery
2.2	Burton Joyce & Bulcote Local History Society	9.15	Mr. J.W. Taylor
2.3	Author	9.16	Author
2.4	LSL (20239-641)	9.17	Mrs. D. Piggott
2,5	Author	9.18	Author
2.6	as 2.2	9.19	Author
3.1	LSL (92734)	9.20	Author
3.2	LSL (Roulstone)	9.21	Mr. J.R. Jeffery
3.3	Author	9.22	Mr. J.R. Jeffery
3.4	Author	9.23	Author
3.5	Author	9.24	Author
3.6	Mr. G.B. Stokes	9.25	Mrs. S.J. Green
3.7	Mrs. J.M. Squires	9.26	Author
3.8	LSL Map of Calverton (1780)	9.27	Mr. J.R. Jeffery
3.9	Author	9.28	Author
3.10	NA (DC/BA/4/2/24}	9.29	Mrs. P.F. Heathcote
4.1	Nottm. Observer October 1957	10.1	Author
4.2	as 4.1	10.2	A.J. Loughton (Dean & Chapter, Southwell Minister
4.3	Author	10.3	LSL (Roulstone)
4.4	NA (C/QDLV/4/1/17)	10.4	Author
5.1	LSL (Roulstone)	11.1	Mr. & Mrs. D & M. Bagley
5.2	LSL (Edwardian Notts. Collection 47932)	11.2	Mr. & Mrs. D & M. Bagley
7.1	Author	11.3	Author
7.2	Author	11.4	Author
7.3	Morris Directory (1869), p.108.	11.5	Author
8.1	Author	11.6	Mr. Levers
8.2	NA (DC/BA/4/2/24)	11.7	Author
8.3	Mrs. S.J. Green	11.8	Mr. & Mrs. D & M. Bagley
8.4	OS 1884 Notts. Sheet XXXV111	11.9	Author
8.5	LSL (35mm Negative 3714)	12.1	Mrs. L. Grice
9.1	Author	Page 78	Mr. & Mrs. B.V. & P.F. Heathcote
9.2	NA (C/PS/NG/3/2)	Inside Back Cover	Mrs. N.J. Rae
9.3	Mr. G. Smith	Back Cover	Mr. & Mrs. B.V. & P.F. Heathcote
9.4	Author		
9.5	Author		
9.6	Nottm. Review (20 August 1833), p.2.f.		
9.7	LSL Tommy Lawton (L79.2)		
9.8	LSL William Derbyshire {L98)		
9.9	Mrs. P. Wyler		

Abbreviations

LSL = Local Studies Library, Nottingham Central Library

NA = Nottinghamshire Archives

Nottinghamshire Archives: references to the plans of public houses

Plan No.	Reference	Plan No.	Reference	Plan No.	Reference	Plan No.	Reference
1	PS/B/34/22/1	7	PS/B/34/58/2	13	DC/SW/4/7/2	19	PS/B/34/97/1
2	DC/BA/4/1/1	8	DC/BA/4/1/1	14	DC/SW/4/7/2	20	DC/BA/4/2/3
3	PS/B/62/8	9	PS/B/26/13	15	DC/SW/4/6/6	21	DC/BA/4/1/1
4	DC/BA/4/1/1	10	PS/B/28/11	16	DC/SW/4/7/2		
5	DC/SW/4/7/2	11	PS/B/34/67/1	17	DC/SW/4/6/21		
6	PS/B/34/32	12	C/PS/NG/3/7	18	PS/B/34/78		

References

1. N.J. (11 July 1812), p.2.c.
2. N.R. (28 June 1844), p.4.f.
3. Burton Joyce & Bulcote Remembered, The Burton Joyce. Local History Group, Burton Joyce (1981), p.20.
4. N.A. In: Alehouse Licences, C/PS/NG/3/5 (1892-02).
5. N.W.E. (I February 1901), p.4.c.
6. N.J. (2 July 1808), p.2.c.
7. N.M. (10 July 1846), p.353.d.
8. N.M. (9 April 1847), p.5.c.
9. N.M. (5 June 1845), p.314.e.
10. N.J. (29 March 1783), p.3.c.
11. N. A. In: Quarter Sessions, QSM/1/32 (19 April 1784).
12. N.A. In: Quarter Sessions, QSM/1/34 (10 September 1799).
13. N.J. (13 June 1789), p.4.c.
14. N.J. (10 January 1795), p.3.c
15. N.A. DDRL 34/40 (9 October 1835).
16. N.R. (8 January 1847), p.4.f.
17. N.A.A. DDSK 113/1 (7 July 1780).
18. NA. DDSK 113/13 (28 January 1788).
19. N.A. DDSK 113/15 & 16 (24 & 25 March 1788).
20. A.N.C (29 September 1759), p.3.a.
21. N.J. (20 February 1773), p.3.a.
22. N.J. (27 November 1773), p.2.d.
23. N.J. (2 September 1797), p.3.a.
24. N.M. (27 August 1831), p.1.c.
25. N.M. (15 September 1832), p.1.b.
26. N.R. (29 August 1851), p.4.f.
27. J. Sharpe, Dick Turpin The Myth of the English Highwayman, Profile Books, London (2004).
28. W. H. Ainsworth, Rookwood, BibloBazaar, (reprint of 1834 edition 2008).
29. L. Mellard, Nottingham in the Days of Dick Turpin, pages from a local diary two centuries ago, (a pamphlet 1924).
30. K.T. Hartlett, N.A. M 11,237
31. N.R. (26 September 1856), p.5.f.
32. N.A. In: Alehouse Recognizances QDLv (1811).
33. N.J. (11 November 1815), p.2.b.
34. A. Sharpe & J. O'Neil, Not Forgetting Caythorpe, Trent Valley Local History Group, Burton Joyce (1992).
35. N.R. (15 June 1849), p.5.e.
36. N.R. (6 July 1849), p.6.d.
37. N.R. In: Alehouse Recognizances, QDLv (1811).
38. N.M. (1 June 1849), p.5.e.
39. N.J. (12 February 1785), p.3.c.
40. N.J. (20 December 1783), p.4.c.
41. N.A. In: Alehouse Recognizance QDLv (1813).
42. N.J. (1 March 1839), p.3.d.
43. N.A. In: Alehouse Licences. C/PS/NG/3/6 (1903-48).
44. N.J. (25 August 1781), p.3.b.
45. N.J. (21 February 1795), p.3.a.
46. N.J. (1 August 1801), p.3.b.
47. N.J. (20 February 1813), p.3.b.
48. N.A. In: Quarter Sessions QSM/1/79/2 (1716).
49. N. A. In: Quarter Sessions, QSM/1/79/2 (1725).
50. N.J. (28 September 1782), p.3.a.
51. N.J. (28 September 1808), p.2.
52. N.J. (2 April 1774), p.3.a.
53. N.A. In: Quarter Sessions, QSM/1/30 (1774).
54. N.J. (21 January 1775), p.3.a.
55. A.N.C. (12 September 1761), p.2.c.
56. N.J. (22 June 1799), p.3.b.
57. N.J. (6 April 1816), p.2.c.
58. N.J. (28 February 1834), p.1.b.
59. N.R. (20 August 1847), p.4e.
60. N.M. (4 February 1832), p.1. d.
61. N.A. Deed of Sale, M7452, (21 August 1818).
62. B. V. Heathcote, Viewing the Lifeless Body, Notts. County Council, Nottingham (2005), p.60.
63. NA. In: Beerhouse Licences C/PS/NG/3/2 (1872-77)
64. N.G. (11 February 1948), p.2.b.
65. N.R. (26 November 1852), p.5.d.
66. N.J. (25 September 1865), p.2.e.
67. N.A. In: Alehouse Licences C/PS/NG/3/5 (1902-03).
68. N.A. In: Beerhouse Licences C/PS/NG/3/2 (1872-77).
69. N.A. In: Beerhouse Licences C/PS/NG/3/24 (1878-91).
70. N.E.P. (16 February 1950), p.3.d.
71. N.M. (12 September 1835), p.1.c.
72. N.J. (22 April 1853), p.5.d.
73. N.R. (20 February 1835), p.2.e.
74. G. Wright & B.J. Curtis, The Inns & Pubs of Nottinghamshire, Nottinghamshire County Council, Nottingham, (1995), p.59.
75. N.R. (30 August 1833), p.2.f.
76. N.M. (8 February 1850), p.5.b.
77. N.M. (1 January 1851), p.4.d.
78. N.J. (15 May 1857), p.5.c.
79. N.R. (21 August 1857), p.5.c.
80. N.A. In: Church Wardens Accounts for Lowdham PR. 1777-8 (1783-1828).
81. N.A. Deed of sale, DD 933/3/4 (1868).
82. N.M. (25 December 1846), p.8.b.
83. N.A. In: Quarter Sessions, QSM/1/32 (31 March & 6 October 1788).
84. N.J. (5 December 1807), p.2.d.
85. N.A. PS/B/7/7 (6 March 1920).
86. N.R. (6 September 1854), p.4.d.
87. N.A. In: Quarter Sessions, QSM/1/33 (28 May 1794).
88. N.J. (5 March 1808), p.2.e.
89. N.J. (5 June 1773), p.3.a.
90. N.J. (18 June 1785), p.3.b.
91. N.J. (24 April 1790), p.3.a.
92. N.J. (6 October 1787), p.2.d.
93. N.J. (27 December 1806), p.2 b.
94. T. Shipside, I Lived in a Village, Woolston Book Co. Nottingham, (1956), p.63.
95. N.J. (9 December 1797), p.3.c.
96. N.A. Indenture, DDSK 63/1 (30 November 1798).
97. N.J. (25 January 1806), p.2.b.
98. N.J. (17 December 1808), p.2.e.
99. N.J. (29 December 1810), p.2.b.
100. N.J. (24 March 1810), p.1.d.
101. N.R. (3 November 1854), p.5.e.
102. N.A. In: Beerhouse Licences C/PS/NG/3/6 (1 May 1929).

References (cont.)

103. N.A. In: Beerhouse Licences C/PS/NG/3/6 (6 March 1837).

104. Whites Directory of Nottinghamshire (1865).

105. N.A. In: Beerhouse Licences C/PS/NG/3/2 (1869).

106. N.A. In: Beerhouse Licences C/PS/NG/3/4 (1887).

107. N.A. In: Beerhouse Licences C/PS/NG/3/4 (1880).

108. N.A. In: Beerhouse Licences C/PS/NG/3/6 (1916).

109. N.W.C. (13 February 1762), p.2.b.

110. N.J. (18 May 1771), p.3.b.

111. N.A. PS/B/7/8 (1853).

112. N.A. PS/B/7/8 (10 August 1872).

113. N.A. In Beerhouse Licences C/PS/NG/3/6 (1 April 1922).

114. N.A. In Alehouse Recognizances. QDLv 4/1/-5/2 (1923).

115. N.M. (10 February 1838), p.44.c.

116. N.R. (4 July 1845), p.3.c.

117. N.A. In: Quarter Sessions, QSM/1/79/4 (1794).

118. N.A. Sale Catalogue for Four Bells, DDHS 103b.

119. N.R. (20 September 1839), p.3.d.

120. N.A. In: Beerhouse Licences,C/PS/NG/3/2.

121. N.A. In: Alehouse Licences C/PS/NG/3/1 (1874).

122. Whites Directory of Nottinghamshire (1853).

123. N.A. DDPF 156/180 (23 August 1861).

124. N. A. In Alehouse Licences C/PS/NG/3/6 (23 February 1926).

125. N.J. (20 February 1796), p.3.a.

126. N.A. In: Alehouse Licences C/PS/NG/3/6 (23 February 1906).

127. N.R. (31 January 1845), p.5.e.

128. N.R. (7 September 1866), p.5.b.

Abbreviations:

A.N.C. = Ayscough's Nottingham Journal

N.A. = Nottinghamshire Archives

N.E.P. = Nottingham Evening Post

N.G. = Nottingham Guardian

N.J. = Nottingham Journal

N.M. = Nottingham Mercury

N.R. = Nottingham Review

N.W.C. = Nottingham Weekly Courant

N.W.E. = Nottinghamshire Weekly Express

Acknowledgements

I would like to thank the staff of the Local Studies Library, Nottingham Central Library for their cheerful co-operation over the period of my research and especially Dorothy J. Ritchie, for her assistance in helping to select the illustrations from their collection. I also acknowledge the help and courtesy I received from the staff of the Nottinghamshire Archives. I very much appreciate the expert help and guidance that has been cheerfully given by my friend Dennis Apple in reading the proof, correcting my typographical errors and helping to solve my computer problems. I am also grateful to Mr. G.B. Stokes, Mrs. J.M. Squires, Mrs. S.J. Green, Mr, G. Smith, Mrs. P. Wyler, Mr. J.R. Jeffery, Mr. J.W. Taylor, Mr. A. Pearce, Mrs D. Piggott, Mr. & Mrs. D. & M. Bagley, Mr. Levers and Mrs. L. Grice for providing me with copies of photographs for publication. My thanks also to Mrs. N.J. Rae for providing me with her sketch map of South Nottinghamshire which is reproduced on the inside back cover. Also every effort has been made to contact others who may own the copyright of images in order to seek their permission to include them in this publication.

Other recent books by Bernard & Pauline Heathcote

(a) Pioneers of Photography in Nottinghamshire 1841-1910 (2001).
(b) A Faithful Likeness: The First Photographic Portrait Studios in the British Isles 1841-55 (2002).
(c) Viewing the Lifeless Body: A Coroner and his inquests held in Nottinghamshire Public Houses during the Nineteenth Century 1828 to 1866 (2005).
(d) Vale of Belvoir Angels: A Survey of a Group of Early Slate Headstones with Characteristic Features which are to be found in the Churchyards of the Vale and some surrounding parishes of Leicestershire, Lincolnshire & Nottinghamshire (2009).